EVOLVING SELF

The Continuous Journey of Becoming

By

Dr. Hesham Mohamed Elsherif

ABOUT THE AUTHOR

Dr. Hesham Mohamed Elsherif stands at the forefront of library management and research, boasting an impressive 22-year tenure in the field. Holding dual doctoral degrees, one in Management and Organizational Leadership and the other in Information Systems and Technology, Dr. Elsherif brings a unique blend of knowledge to any intellectual endeavor.

An expert in Empirical research methodology, Dr. Elsherif specializes particularly in the Qualitative approach and Action research. This specialization has not only strengthened his research endeavors but has also allowed him to contribute invaluable insights and advancements in these areas.

Over the years, Dr. Elsherif has made significant contributions to the academic world not only as a professional researcher but also as an Adjunct Professor. This multifaceted role in the educational landscape has further solidified his reputation as a thought leader and pioneer.

Furthermore, Dr. Elsherif's expertise isn't confined to one region. He has served as a consultant to numerous educational institutions on an international scale, sharing best practices, innovative strategies, and his deep insights into the ever-evolving realms of management and technology.

Combining a passion for education with an unparalleled depth of knowledge, Dr. Elsherif continues to inspire, educate, and lead in both the library and academic communities.

PREFACE

Welcome to "Evolving Self: The Continuous Journey of Becoming," a book that aims to be both a companion and a guide on the winding path of personal growth and self-discovery. This book is an invitation to explore the deepest layers of your being, to understand the dynamics of change, and to embrace the continuous process of becoming that defines the human experience.

The Genesis of This Book

This book was born out of a series of questions that have intrigued me for years: How do we grow and change? What drives our evolution as individuals? How do we navigate the challenges and transitions that shape our lives? In seeking answers, I found that the journey of the evolving self is not just a psychological process but a holistic one, encompassing emotional, intellectual, social, and spiritual dimensions.

Navigating the Journey

Through these pages, we will embark on a journey that takes us through the landscapes of change and stability, challenge and triumph. The book is structured to reflect the various stages of personal development, each stage presenting its own set of challenges and opportunities. We will delve into the dynamics of internal growth, the influence of external factors, and the importance of self-awareness and reflection in facilitating our evolution.

A Book for Everyone

Whether you are at a crossroads in life, seeking to understand past experiences, or simply curious about the nature of personal growth, this book is for you. It is written for those who aspire to a deeper understanding of themselves and for those who seek to foster growth in others – be it as parents, educators, mentors, or leaders.

A Personal Invitation

As you read "Evolving Self: The Continuous Journey of Becoming," I encourage you to engage with the content actively. Reflect on your experiences, question your beliefs, and consider new perspectives. This book is not just a collection of ideas but a starting point for introspection and dialogue – with yourself and with the world around you.

In Conclusion

The journey of the evolving self is endless and ever-changing. It is my hope that this book serves as a valuable resource and a source of inspiration as you navigate the complexities and the beauties of your personal journey of becoming.

With warm regards,

Dr. Hesham Mohamed Elsherif

WHO SHOULD READ THIS BOOK?

Evolving Self: The Continuous Journey of Becoming" is a book that resonates with a wide spectrum of readers, each at different stages in their life's journey. It is designed to offer insights, guidance, and inspiration to anyone interested in personal growth and self-discovery. Here are some groups of people who will find particular value in this book:

1. **Self-Help Enthusiasts:**

- If you are someone who is always seeking to understand yourself better, to grow, and to improve, this book is for you. It provides a nuanced look at personal development, going beyond surface-level advice.

2. **Professionals in Transition:**

- For those experiencing changes in their career or personal life, this book offers a framework to understand and navigate these transitions more effectively.

3. **Young Adults:**

- As you stand at the threshold of multiple life choices, this book can be a guiding light, helping you understand the processes of change and self-formation.

4. **Parents and Educators:**

- If you are involved in guiding others, especially young minds, this book can enhance your understanding of personal development and how to foster it in others.

5. **Therapists, Coaches, and Counselors:**

- Professionals working in the realm of personal development and mental health will find valuable insights into the evolving nature of the self, which can enrich their practice.

6. **Anyone Facing Life Challenges:**

- If you are going through a tough phase and looking for ways to cope and grow, this book offers perspectives that can provide comfort and direction.

7. **Spiritual Seekers:**

- Those on a spiritual path will appreciate the book's exploration of the evolving self, including its spiritual dimensions.

8. **Curious Minds:**

- If you are someone who is always curious about human nature, psychology, and the art of living, this book provides a wealth of knowledge and food for thought.

9. **Leaders and Managers:**

- Understanding the journey of personal growth can be crucial in leading and managing others effectively, making this book a valuable resource for those in leadership positions.

10. **Retirees and Senior Citizens:**

- Those in the later stages of life looking to reflect on their journey and continue their personal growth will find this book both affirming and enlightening.

"Evolving Self: The Continuous Journey of Becoming" is more than just a book; it's a companion for anyone interested in exploring the depths of their own growth and the potential for change within themselves. It's for those who believe that the journey of self-discovery and evolution is a lifelong pursuit, filled with lessons, challenges, and triumphs.

Welcome to a journey of self-evolution.

Dr. Hesham Mohamed Elsherif

WHY THIS BOOK IS ESSENTIAL READING?

In a world that is rapidly changing and increasingly complex, understanding the nature of personal growth and evolution is more important than ever. "Evolving Self: The Continuous Journey of Becoming" is not just another self-help book; it is a vital guide to understanding and navigating the intricate process of personal development. Here's why this book is essential reading:

1. **Holistic Approach to Personal Growth:**

- This book offers a comprehensive view of personal development, covering emotional, intellectual, social, and spiritual dimensions. This holistic perspective is essential in understanding the complete picture of self-evolution.

2. **Navigating Life Transitions:**

- Whether you are entering adulthood, mid-life, or the golden years, life transitions can be challenging. This book provides insights and strategies to manage these changes effectively, making it a valuable resource at any life stage.

3. **Empowerment through Self-Understanding:**

- By deepening your understanding of yourself and the nature of change, you gain the power to steer your life in the direction you desire. This book empowers readers by equipping them with the knowledge and tools for self-realization.

4. **Enhancing Relationships and Communication:**

- Understanding the evolving self also improves your ability to relate to others. This book offers insights into interpersonal dynamics, enhancing your empathy and communication skills.

5. **Adaptability in a Fast-Paced World:**

- In our fast-paced, ever-changing world, adaptability is key to success and well-being. This book teaches the art of adaptability, helping you to thrive in any situation.

6. **Support for Mental and Emotional Health:**

- Recognizing and navigating the complexities of your inner world is crucial for mental and emotional health. This book provides a supportive framework for dealing with various psychological challenges.

7. **Inspiration for Lifelong Learning:**

- "Evolving Self" promotes the idea of lifelong learning and self-improvement. It inspires you to continually seek knowledge, growth, and personal development.

8. **Guidance for Purposeful Living:**

- If you're seeking a more meaningful and purposeful life, this book offers valuable guidance. It helps you align your actions with your deeper values and goals.

9. **Resource for Professionals:**

- Therapists, coaches, educators, and leaders will find this book an invaluable resource in understanding and facilitating growth in others.

10. **Catalyst for Positive Change:**

- This book is not just about understanding change; it's about implementing it. It acts as a catalyst for making positive changes in your life and the lives of those around you.

"Evolving Self: The Continuous Journey of Becoming" is essential reading for anyone who wants to engage deeply with the process of personal growth. It offers a rich blend of theoretical insights and practical wisdom, making it a timeless resource for personal evolution.

Embrace the journey of becoming your best self.

Dr. Hesham Mohamed Elsherif

Table of Contents

PART I: UNDERSTANDING THE JOURNEY

Chapter 1: The Nature of Change

The idea of the "Evolving Self" in the context of personal development and psychology refers to the ongoing process of growth and change that individuals experience throughout their lives. This concept acknowledges that human beings are continuously in a state of becoming, adapting, and transforming in response to their experiences, environments, and internal changes.

The Nature of Change:

1. **Dynamic and Non-linear Process:**

   - Change is not a straightforward or linear process. It often involves cycles of progress, regression, learning, and adaptation.

   - Individuals may find themselves revisiting previous stages of development or encountering similar challenges in new forms.

2. **Influenced by Internal and External Factors:**

   - Internal factors include psychological aspects such as beliefs, values, emotions, and cognitive processes.

   - External factors encompass social, environmental, cultural, and economic influences that can shape one's path of development.

3. **Holistic Development:**

   - Holistic development encompasses physical, emotional, intellectual, social, and spiritual growth.

   - Each of these areas can affect and reinforce the others, contributing to the overall evolution of the self.

4. **Stages and Transitions:**

   - Life is marked by stages (childhood, adolescence, adulthood, etc.) and transitions between these stages.

- These transitions are often periods of significant change and can be catalysts for personal growth and self-redefinition.

5. **Individual Variability:**

   - The journey of becoming is highly individualistic. Each person's path is unique, influenced by their personal history, choices, and circumstances.

   - There is no "one size fits all" in personal development; strategies and paths differ greatly between individuals.

6. **Interplay of Stability and Change:**

   - While change is constant, there is also an element of stability in the evolving self. Core aspects of personality and deep-seated values may remain relatively stable over time.

   - The balance between change and continuity is crucial for a sense of identity.

7. **The Role of Reflection and Self-Awareness:**

   - Reflection and self-awareness are key in the evolving self. They allow individuals to understand their experiences, learn from them, and make more informed choices.

   - Self-awareness aids in recognizing patterns, strengths, weaknesses, and areas for growth.

8. **Influence of Relationships and Social Interactions:**

   - Relationships and social interactions play a significant role in shaping the evolving self.

   - They provide feedback, mirror aspects of the self, and offer opportunities for learning and development.

Implications for Personal Development

1. **Continuous Learning and Adaptation:**

   - Embracing the concept of the evolving self implies a commitment to lifelong learning and adaptation.

   - This mindset encourages resilience and flexibility in the face of change.

2. **Goal Setting and Reevaluation:**

- Goals may shift as individuals evolve. Regular reevaluation of goals and aspirations is important to ensure they remain aligned with one's evolving self.

3. **Embracing Change as an Opportunity:**

- Viewing change as an opportunity for growth, rather than a threat, is a key perspective in the journey of becoming.

4. **Self-Compassion and Patience:**

- The evolving self requires a degree of self-compassion and patience, recognizing that growth often involves challenges and setbacks.

5. **Seeking Support and Resources:**

- Utilizing support systems, such as friends, family, mentors, or professional help, can be vital in navigating the complexities of personal growth.

The Only Constant:

The axiom "change is the only constant" is profoundly relevant to the concept of the evolving self. This section of "Evolving Self: The Continuous Journey of Becoming" focuses on understanding and embracing this inevitable aspect of life. The nature of change is multifaceted and impacts our journey of personal growth in several ways:

1. **Inherent in Human Experience:**

- Change is an intrinsic part of the human condition. From physiological changes like aging to psychological changes in beliefs and attitudes, our existence is defined by continuous transformation.

- Understanding that change is a fundamental aspect of life can help individuals embrace it as a natural, rather than disruptive, element of their existence.

2. **Psychological Adaptation:**

- Change necessitates psychological adaptation. This adaptation can take various forms, including cognitive reframing, emotional regulation, and behavioral adjustments.

- The evolving self is about developing the psychological tools and resilience to adapt effectively to life's changes.

3. **Growth and Development:**

   - Change is not just about adapting to new circumstances; it's also a driver of personal growth and development. Challenges and new experiences foster learning and self-discovery.

   - The journey of becoming involves leveraging change as an opportunity for growth, even when it appears daunting or unwelcome.

4. **Phases of Life:**

   - Life can be viewed as a series of phases, each with its own set of changes and challenges. From childhood to old age, these phases shape our identity, values, and perspectives.

   - The evolving self is about navigating these phases with awareness and intention, understanding that each phase offers unique opportunities for self-development.

5. **Impact of External Forces:**

   - External forces such as societal shifts, technological advancements, and cultural changes significantly impact our personal journey of becoming.

   - Adapting to these external changes requires flexibility and an openness to reevaluate and update our understanding of ourselves and the world.

6. **Interpersonal Changes:**

   - Changes in relationships, whether through dynamics, losses, or new connections, profoundly affect our sense of self.

   - The evolving self encompasses the ability to grow through these interpersonal changes, learning to form and maintain healthy relationships.

7. **Crisis as Catalyst:**

   - Often, major life crises become powerful catalysts for change. While challenging, these moments can lead to significant personal transformation and growth.

- Recognizing and embracing the potential for positive change in the face of crisis is a key aspect of the evolving self.

8. **Lifelong Process:**

- The evolving self is not a destination but a continuous journey. It acknowledges that change is a lifelong process, with each stage of life offering new lessons and opportunities for growth.

9. **Self-Reflection and Awareness:**

- A critical part of adapting to change is self-reflection and awareness. Understanding one's reactions to change, the patterns in how one adapts, and the outcomes of these adaptations are crucial for intentional growth.

10. **The Balance of Change and Continuity:**

- While change is constant, there is also a need for continuity. Balancing change with a sense of continuity in core values and identity is crucial for a coherent sense of self.

In "Evolving Self: The Continuous Journey of Becoming," understanding and embracing the nature of change is central. Change, as the only constant, is not just a challenge to be managed but a force that propels growth, learning, and personal evolution. By recognizing and adapting to the ever-present nature of change, individuals can navigate their life journey with greater resilience, purpose, and fulfillment.

Historical and Cultural Views on Change:

Understanding the evolving self involves not only personal introspection but also a broader perspective on how change has been perceived and interpreted throughout history and across different cultures. This aspect is crucial as it provides a contextual background against which individual change can be understood.

1. **Historical Perspectives on Change:**

- Throughout history, philosophers, theologians, and scholars have pondered the nature of change. For instance, ancient Greek philosophers like Heraclitus posited that change is the fundamental essence of the universe, famously stating, "No man ever steps in the same river twice."

- In contrast, other philosophies, like those of Parmenides, viewed change as an illusion, with the true nature of reality being unchanging.

- These historical views inform our understanding of change, influencing contemporary perspectives and attitudes toward personal and societal transformation.

2. **Cultural Interpretations of Change:**

- Different cultures have unique ways of understanding and approaching change. For example, many Eastern philosophies, such as Buddhism and Taoism, embrace change as a natural and inevitable part of life and the universe.

- In contrast, some Western cultures have historically been more focused on maintaining stability and status quo, although this has evolved significantly in recent times.

3. **Change in Mythology and Religion:**

- Many mythologies and religions address the concept of change, often through stories of transformation, rebirth, and renewal. These narratives can provide deep insights into how different cultures interpret the process of change and its impact on the human experience.

- For instance, the concept of reincarnation in Hinduism and Buddhism speaks to a continuous cycle of change and evolution of the self.

4. **Impact of Technological and Social Change:**

- The Industrial Revolution, the Digital Revolution, and other major technological and social shifts have dramatically altered how societies view change. These revolutions have shown that change can be rapid, profound, and far-reaching, affecting every aspect of human life.

- Understanding these shifts is crucial in contextualizing personal change within the larger societal and historical context.

5. **Cultural Attitudes Towards Personal Change:**

- Cultural norms and values significantly influence attitudes towards personal growth and change. In some cultures, there is a strong emphasis on self-improvement and personal development, while in others, conformity and adherence to traditional roles are valued.

- Recognizing these cultural influences helps in understanding one's own approach to change and personal growth.

6. **Globalization and Cross-Cultural Exchange:**

   - In today's interconnected world, exposure to diverse cultures and ideas has led to a more complex understanding of change. This cross-cultural exchange has enriched the dialogue about personal and societal transformation.

   - It allows for a more nuanced and comprehensive view of the evolving self, one that incorporates diverse perspectives and experiences.

7. **The Role of History in Personal Change:**

   - An individual's personal history, including their cultural and familial background, shapes their approach to and understanding of change.

   - Historical events, both on a personal and a global scale, can have significant impacts on the trajectory of one's life and development.

In "Evolving Self: The Continuous Journey of Becoming," the exploration of historical and cultural views on change provides a rich tapestry of understanding. This exploration highlights how perceptions of change are deeply embedded in historical, cultural, and philosophical contexts. By acknowledging and integrating these broader perspectives, individuals can gain deeper insights into their personal journeys of change and evolution, appreciating the complexity and diversity of the human experience of change.

Conclusion

The evolving self is a continuous journey of becoming, characterized by a dynamic interplay of change and stability, influenced by a multitude of factors, both internal and external. Understanding and embracing this concept can lead to a more fulfilling and adaptive approach to personal development and life.

Chapter 2: Personal Growth

In "Evolving Self: The Continuous Journey of Becoming," the concept of personal growth is explored as a fundamental and ongoing process, rather than a transient phase or a series of milestones. This comprehensive view underscores the idea that personal development is a lifelong journey, deeply embedded in every aspect of human life.

1. **Defining Personal Growth:**

   - Personal growth encompasses the evolution of one's emotions, thoughts, behaviors, and perceptions. It involves acquiring new understanding, skills, and insights, and applying them to improve oneself and one's interaction with the world.

   - It is a holistic process that includes not just intellectual and skill-based growth but also emotional, spiritual, and social development.

2. **Continuous and Lifelong Process:**

   - Unlike the traditional view that personal growth is limited to certain life stages (like adolescence or mid-life), this book posits that growth is continuous and does not cease at any point in life.

   - Every stage of life, from childhood to old age, presents unique opportunities and challenges for growth, making it an unending journey.

3. **Beyond Developmental Stages:**

   - While psychological theories often focus on specific developmental stages, personal growth extends beyond these confines. It includes learning from experiences, adapting to changes, and continuously refining one's sense of self.

   - Personal growth is dynamic, not restricted to a linear progression tied to age or life stages.

4. **Role of Experiences and Challenges:**

   - Life experiences, both positive and negative, are seen as catalysts for personal growth. Challenges, in particular, can spur significant development, encouraging resilience, adaptability, and self-awareness.

- How individuals respond to and learn from these experiences is a key aspect of their ongoing development.

5. **The Interplay of Internal and External Influences:**

- Personal growth is influenced by a combination of internal factors (like personality, values, and beliefs) and external factors (such as social environment, culture, and life events).

- Understanding this interplay is crucial in recognizing the multifaceted nature of personal growth.

6. **Self-Reflection and Conscious Effort:**

- Conscious self-reflection and effort are vital in the personal growth process. Active engagement in self-discovery and deliberate steps towards self-improvement are essential components of this journey.

- It's about being proactive in one's development, rather than passively experiencing life.

7. **The Role of Relationships:**

- Interpersonal relationships are both a source and a catalyst for personal growth. Through relationships, individuals learn about empathy, compromise, communication, and understanding diverse perspectives.

- Relationships can challenge and encourage individuals to grow in ways they might not in isolation.

8. **Integration of Past Experiences:**

- Personal growth involves integrating past experiences, including successes, failures, joys, and traumas, into one's evolving self-concept.

- This integration helps in developing a more cohesive and authentic sense of self.

9. **Lifelong Learning and Adaptability:**

- Embracing lifelong learning and maintaining adaptability are key aspects of continuous personal growth. This mindset encourages constant evolution and openness to new experiences and ideas.

- It is about remaining curious and open-minded throughout life's journey.

Childhood to Adulthood: The Basic Arc:

In "Evolving Self: The Continuous Journey of Becoming," the transition from childhood to adulthood is examined not just as a developmental phase but as a fundamental arc in the continuum of personal growth. This arc is crucial in laying the foundation for continuous evolution throughout an individual's life.

1. **Childhood: The Formative Years**

   - **Foundations of Self-Concept:** Childhood is where the initial sense of self begins to form. Children learn about who they are, their likes and dislikes, and how they relate to the world around them.

   - **Role of Early Experiences:** Early life experiences, including family dynamics, education, and social interactions, play a significant role in shaping personality, beliefs, and values.

   - **Development of Basic Skills:** Childhood is also about developing basic skills—emotional, social, cognitive, and physical. These skills are the building blocks for future growth.

2. **Adolescence: The Transitional Phase**

   - **Identity Formation:** Adolescence is marked by a quest for identity. Teenagers start to question their childhood beliefs and values, exploring and defining their individual identity.

   - **Emotional and Social Growth:** This period involves significant emotional and social development, with teenagers learning to navigate complex social dynamics and relationships.

   - **Independence and Autonomy:** Adolescents start seeking independence, making choices and decisions that will impact their future selves.

3. **Young Adulthood: Establishing Self**

   - **Consolidation of Identity:** Young adults work on consolidating their identity, often balancing personal aspirations with societal expectations.

   - **Career and Relationships:** Major life choices, such as career paths and romantic partnerships, begin to solidify during this stage.

- **Personal Values and Beliefs:** Young adults develop and refine their personal values and beliefs, influenced by broader experiences outside their family of origin.

4. **Adulthood: Continuous Growth and Adaptation**

- **Life Management:** Adulthood involves managing various aspects of life—work, relationships, family, and personal interests. Balancing these aspects becomes a key growth area.

- **Reevaluation and Mid-Life Transition:** Many adults go through a phase of reevaluating life choices and goals, often leading to significant personal growth and change.

- **Maturity and Wisdom:** Adulthood is an ongoing process of acquiring wisdom, learning from experiences, and adapting to life's changes.

5. **Common Challenges and Growth Opportunities**

- **Navigating Independence:** Moving from dependence to independence is a critical transition, encompassing financial, emotional, and social aspects.

- **Relationship Dynamics:** Changing family dynamics, romantic relationships, and friendships offer opportunities for deep personal growth.

- **Career and Purpose:** Choices about education and career paths are not just practical decisions but also deeply tied to personal growth and self-expression.

6. **Integrating Experiences Across the Arc**

- **Reflective Learning:** Integrating experiences from each stage of life is key to personal growth. Reflection helps in understanding how past experiences shape current beliefs and behaviors.

- **Continuous Development:** The skills, insights, and knowledge gained in earlier stages provide the foundation for facing future challenges and opportunities.

The journey from childhood to adulthood, as presented in "Evolving Self: The Continuous Journey of Becoming," is a foundational arc in the narrative of personal growth. It is more than just a phase; it's a critical period that sets the tone for ongoing development throughout an individual's life. Understanding and reflecting on this arc can provide valuable insights into one's evolving self, emphasizing that personal growth is a dynamic, life-long process.

Beyond Adulthood: The Overlooked Arc:

In "Evolving Self: The Continuous Journey of Becoming," the journey of personal growth extends beyond the traditional focus on early life stages, exploring the often-overlooked arc of development that occurs later in life. This section underscores the importance of recognizing and embracing growth opportunities in the stages beyond adulthood.

1. **Middle Age: The Age of Reflection and Transition**

   - **Reassessment of Life Choices:** Middle age often prompts individuals to reflect on their life choices, achievements, and future aspirations. This period can be a significant turning point, leading to profound personal growth.

   - **Shifting Priorities:** As individuals experience changes in career, family dynamics, and physical abilities, there is often a shift in priorities, emphasizing personal fulfillment, relationships, and leisure.

   - **Coping with Change:** Dealing with changes such as aging parents, children leaving home, or career transitions, middle-aged individuals often develop new coping strategies and resilience.

2. **Late Adulthood: Continued Growth and Wisdom**

   - **Embracing Aging:** Late adulthood involves coming to terms with aging and its implications. Acceptance and adaptation to these changes are key aspects of personal growth during this stage.

   - **Legacy and Contribution:** Many individuals focus on legacy—how they wish to contribute to their families, communities, and society. This can lead to engaging in mentoring, volunteering, or other forms of social contribution.

   - **Deepening of Relationships:** Relationships often take on deeper significance, with a focus on quality and meaningful connections.

3. **Retirement: A New Phase of Exploration**

- **Redefining Identity Beyond Work:** Retirement provides an opportunity to explore aspects of identity beyond professional roles. It can be a time for pursuing interests and passions that were previously sidelined.

- **Adjustment to New Lifestyle:** Adapting to the changes in daily routines and lifestyle post-retirement is a significant aspect of personal growth, often requiring a re-evaluation of self and purpose.

4. **Elderly Years: Wisdom and Integration**

- **Integration of Life Experiences:** The elderly years offer a unique perspective, allowing individuals to integrate and reflect upon their life experiences. This integration can lead to a profound sense of wisdom and contentment.

- **Facing Mortality:** Coming to terms with mortality is a profound aspect of growth in this stage, often leading to heightened spiritual awareness or existential reflection.

- **Passing on Knowledge and Experience:** Many find fulfillment in passing on their knowledge, wisdom, and experiences to younger generations, contributing to their legacy.

5. **Challenges and Growth Opportunities**

- **Health and Physical Changes:** Navigating health issues and physical changes is a major aspect of growth in later life stages, often requiring adjustments in self-perception and lifestyle.

- **Social Roles and Relationships:** Changes in social roles, such as becoming a grandparent or a widow(er), affect personal identity and provide opportunities for growth and new experiences.

- **Cognitive Changes:** Adapting to and coping with cognitive changes is an important aspect of personal development in these stages.

6. **Lifelong Learning and Adaptation**

- **Continued Learning:** The pursuit of learning and new experiences should not cease with age. Engaging in new hobbies, education, or travel can enrich life and foster continued growth.

- **Adapting to Life's Cycles:** Understanding and adapting to the cyclical nature of life, with its gains and losses, is key to growth in these stages.

The stages of life beyond adulthood are rich with opportunities for continued personal growth, as highlighted in "Evolving Self: The Continuous Journey of Becoming." This part of the journey, often neglected in discussions about personal development, is crucial for a comprehensive understanding of the evolving self. It emphasizes that growth and development are not confined to the early years but are integral, ongoing processes throughout the entire lifespan

Conclusion

In the context of "Evolving Self: The Continuous Journey of Becoming," personal growth is viewed as an enduring and integral part of life, not confined to any specific phase or period. It is a complex, dynamic process that involves a continuous reevaluation and reinvention of the self. By embracing this perspective, individuals can approach life with a mindset geared towards ongoing development, learning, and self-improvement, making the most of the journey of becoming.

Chapter 3: The Psyche's Structure

In "Evolving Self: The Continuous Journey of Becoming," the exploration of the psyche's structure is akin to a journey into a vast and intricate landscape, where every element plays a crucial role in shaping the overall terrain of personal growth and self-understanding.

1. **The Psyche as a Multilayered Entity:**

   - Imagine the psyche as a complex, multi-layered structure, akin to a grand mansion with various floors, rooms, and hidden passages. Each layer, from the conscious to the unconscious, holds different aspects of our being, from our most immediate thoughts to our deepest, unacknowledged emotions.

2. **The Conscious Mind: The Upper Floors:**

   - The conscious mind is like the upper floors of the mansion, well-lit and familiar. Here reside our active thoughts, decisions, and perceptions—the parts of our mental processes that we can easily access and recognize. This is where we spend most of our waking moments, making conscious choices, and engaging with the world around us.

3. **The Subconscious Mind: The Ground Floor:**

   - Below this is the ground floor, representing the subconscious mind. It's less visible but still accessible if we take the time to explore. This area holds our recently stored memories, learned skills, and beliefs that we don't actively think about but that subtly influence our behavior and emotional reactions.

4. **The Unconscious Mind: The Basement:**

   - Deep below lies the basement, the realm of the unconscious mind. It's a place we rarely visit consciously, but it stores the core of our deepest fears, desires, and repressed experiences. These hidden elements shape our fundamental beliefs about ourselves and the world, often in ways we're not directly aware of.

5. **The Development of the Psyche: Building the Structure:**

- The building of this mansion begins in childhood. Early experiences lay the foundation and construct the basic structure. As we grow, each experience, each lesson, and each emotional encounter adds a brick, a room, or a new wing to this mansion.

6. **Navigating the Psyche: A Lifelong Exploration:**

   - Understanding oneself is akin to exploring this vast mansion. We may find ourselves in familiar rooms (conscious thoughts) or wandering into less frequented areas (subconscious). Occasionally, we might stumble upon a hidden door leading to the basement (unconscious), revealing insights that were previously obscured.

7. **Therapeutic Exploration: Guided Tours of the Psyche:**

   - Psychotherapy and counseling can be seen as guided tours of this mansion. Therapists help us navigate the more complex, less understood areas, assisting us in making sense of what we find there and how it influences our 'above ground' life.

8. **External Influences: The World Outside the Mansion:**

   - The world outside the mansion - our social, cultural, and environmental contexts - continually impacts the structure. These influences can be like the weather, sometimes bright and supportive, other times stormy and challenging, shaping the mansion's evolution.

9. **The Evolving Psyche: Renovation and Reconstruction:**

   - As we grow and evolve, our psyche's structure is not static. We renovate old rooms and sometimes reconstruct entire sections as our beliefs, values, and understandings change. This ongoing process of renovation and reconstruction is central to the journey of becoming.

Conclusion

The narrative of the psyche in "Evolving Self: The Continuous Journey of Becoming" paints a vivid picture of a dynamic, evolving structure. This conceptualization helps to understand that personal growth involves exploring and understanding various layers of our consciousness. It's a continual process of discovery, understanding, and sometimes, transformation of the deepest parts of ourselves. As we journey through this mansion, we learn, we grow, and we become more attuned to the intricate complexities of our inner world.

The Conscious and Unconscious:

The exploration of the psyche's structure, particularly the interplay between the conscious and unconscious realms, is akin to embarking on a deep-sea voyage, where the surface waters and the depths below tell a story of a complex, interconnected world.

1. **The Conscious Mind: The Ocean's Surface**

   - Picture the conscious mind as the surface of a vast ocean. This is where the sunlight hits, where you can see the ripples and waves caused by the wind — the immediate, visible happenings. The ocean's surface represents our conscious experiences: thoughts we are aware of, decisions we make deliberately, and actions we take knowingly.

   - As a sailor navigates these waters, we navigate our day-to-day life through the conscious mind, handling tasks, engaging in conversations, and making choices based on what we see and know.

2. **The Unconscious Mind: The Depths Below**

   - Beneath this surface lies the vast and mysterious world of the deep ocean — the unconscious mind. It's a realm filled with wonders and terrors, ancient wrecks, and undiscovered creatures. It holds our deepest fears, long-forgotten memories, and primal desires. These are elements of our psyche that we are not directly aware of but influence us in profound ways.

   - Just as the ocean's depths affect the life at the surface, our unconscious mind shapes our behaviors, reactions, and even life patterns without our immediate awareness.

3. **The Interplay: A Voyage of Discovery**

   - The journey of personal growth involves diving into these depths. Like a deep-sea diver, we must equip ourselves with the right tools — self-reflection, therapy, mindfulness — to explore this underwater world safely and effectively.

   - In this exploration, we might discover submerged treasures — hidden strengths and talents or insights into our deepest motivations. We might also encounter and confront the more menacing creatures of our psyche: repressed emotions, unresolved conflicts, and deep-seated fears.

4. **Navigating the Unconscious: Encountering the Unknown**

- Exploring the unconscious can be daunting, like navigating a realm where the rules of the surface world do not always apply. Here, symbols and dreams become our guideposts, and intuition is as important as rational thought.

- This exploration is not just about discovery but also about integration. It's about bringing to the surface what we find in the depths, understanding it, and integrating it into our conscious life. This process enriches and deepens our self-understanding.

5. **The Role of External Forces: Currents and Tides**

- Just as ocean currents and tides are influenced by external forces like the moon and weather, our psyche is influenced by external factors — our environment, culture, and relationships. These forces can bring to the surface aspects of our unconscious or push our conscious experiences deeper into the depths.

6. **The Continuous Journey: Evolving Self-Awareness**

- The voyage between the conscious and unconscious is not a one-time journey. It is a continuous process of discovery, understanding, and integration. As we evolve, the boundaries between these realms shift, unveiling new layers of our psyche and new territories of our inner world.

In "Evolving Self: The Continuous Journey of Becoming," the narrative of the psyche's structure, encompassing both the conscious and unconscious realms, is akin to a perpetual voyage across and beneath the ocean's surface. It's a journey of constant learning and interaction between what is seen and what lies beneath, providing a profound and nuanced understanding of our evolving selves. This metaphorical voyage underlines the depth and complexity of personal growth, emphasizing the importance of exploring both the visible and hidden aspects of our psyche.

Dreams, Symbols, and the Inner Self:

The realm of dreams and symbols offers a rich and vivid narrative for exploring the intricacies of the psyche and the inner self. This exploration is akin to entering a mystic forest, a place of mystery and profound truths, where every element holds significance, and every path leads to deeper self-discovery.

1. **Dreams: The Mystic Forest of the Psyche**

   - Imagine each dream as a journey into a mystical forest, a symbolic representation of the psyche's deeper realms. In this forest, the conscious mind rests, and the subconscious and unconscious layers communicate through symbols and narratives.

   - These dreams are not random; they are the psyche's way of processing, integrating, and communicating internal conflicts, desires, fears, and aspirations. Like a forest, they can be enchanting or intimidating, revealing hidden treasures or concealed dangers.

2. **Symbols: The Language of the Inner Self**

   - Within this forest, symbols are the language. A river in a dream might represent emotional flow or barriers, while a key may symbolize a solution or secret. These symbols are unique to each individual – their personal mythology developed through their life experiences, cultural background, and personal associations.

   - Deciphering this symbolic language is a process of self-discovery. It requires patience and introspection, as the same symbol can hold different meanings at different times, depending on the context and the individual's current life situation.

3. **Navigating the Dream Forest: Exploring the Unconscious**

   - As one navigates this dream forest, they encounter various aspects of themselves – some familiar, others alien or forgotten. These encounters, though sometimes unsettling, are opportunities for growth and understanding.

   - The journey through the dream forest is not linear. It twists and turns, with paths doubling back, mirroring the complexity and non-linearity of personal growth and the evolving self.

4. **The Role of Reflection and Interpretation**

   - Reflecting upon and interpreting dreams is like sitting by a campfire in the forest, pondering the day's journey. It involves examining the emotions, actions, and symbols encountered in the dream and connecting them to waking life.

- This reflection can lead to insights about unresolved issues, hidden fears, and desires, or aspects of the self that need attention or expression.

5. **Integration: Bringing Lessons from the Forest into the Light**

- The ultimate goal of exploring this mystic forest of dreams is integration. It's about bringing the insights, lessons, and messages from the unconscious into the conscious mind, leading to a more holistic understanding of oneself.

- This integration is a key aspect of personal growth, as it fosters a deeper connection between the conscious and unconscious parts of the psyche, leading to greater harmony and self-awareness.

6. **Continual Journey: Evolving Through Dreams and Symbols**

- The journey through this forest is ongoing. Each night, new dreams offer fresh perspectives, and each interpretation adds another layer to the understanding of the self.

- The evolving self is thus in a constant dialogue with its inner world, where dreams and symbols play a crucial role in facilitating personal growth and self-discovery.

Conclusion

In the narrative of dreams and symbols as pathways to understanding the inner self is both mystical and profound. It presents a captivating exploration of the deeper layers of the psyche, where dreams are not just figments of the imagination, but meaningful communications from our innermost selves. This journey into the symbolic forest of the psyche is an essential part of the continuous journey of becoming, revealing the ever-evolving landscape of the human soul

Chapter 4: Nature vs. Nurture: Their Roles in our Evolution

The journey of personal evolution, the continuous shaping and reshaping of the self, is a fascinating interplay between two powerful forces: nature and nurture. This narrative delves into how these elements intertwine in the ongoing process of becoming, highlighting the complexity and beauty of human development.

The Genesis of Self: Nature's Blueprint

The story begins with nature, the genetic inheritance that lays the foundation of who we are. Encoded in the DNA are the blueprints of physical attributes, predispositions to certain health conditions, and even aspects of our temperament and cognitive abilities. This genetic endowment is like the first brushstroke on a canvas, setting a basic outline.

- **Physical Attributes**: Height, eye color, and other physical traits are largely determined by genetics.

- **Health Dispositions**: Propensities for certain diseases, like diabetes or heart conditions, are often inherited.

- **Temperament and Intelligence**: Even certain personality traits and elements of intelligence have a genetic component.

The Canvas Expands: Nurture Shapes the Journey

As significant as nature is, it is just the beginning. Nurture plays a crucial role in filling out the picture. This encompasses the environment we grow up in: our family, cultural background, education, and the myriad experiences that life presents.

- **Family Influence**: The values, beliefs, and behaviors learned from family shape attitudes and moral frameworks.

- **Cultural Context**: Cultural norms and practices influence our worldview and social interactions.

- **Educational Experiences**: Education molds critical thinking, knowledge acquisition, and skill development.

- **Life Experiences**: Personal experiences, both positive and negative, profoundly affect emotional growth and resilience.

The Interplay of Nature and Nurture: A Dynamic Dance

The most fascinating aspect of personal evolution is how nature and nurture are not isolated forces but interact in complex ways.

- **Gene-Environment Interaction**: Certain genetic potentials may be activated or suppressed depending on environmental factors. For instance, a genetic propensity for musical talent may only manifest if the individual is exposed to music training.

- **Epigenetics**: Life experiences can cause changes in how genes are expressed, without altering the genetic code itself. This epigenetic modification illustrates how nurture can influence nature.

- **Adaptive Behaviors**: As individuals navigate their environment, they develop behaviors that may seem to override genetic predispositions. A person genetically inclined to high anxiety might learn coping mechanisms that mitigate this trait.

Personal Evolution Over a Lifetime

The journey of becoming is continuous and lifelong. As people age, they gather more experiences, their environments change, and they constantly reinterpret their innate dispositions.

- **Childhood and Adolescence**: This is a period of rapid physical and psychological development, where nurture heavily influences identity formation.

- **Adulthood**: As adults, individuals have more autonomy in shaping their environment, allowing for a renegotiation of the balance between nature and nurture.

- **Later Life**: In later years, reflections on past experiences often lead to a deeper understanding of the self, harmonizing genetic predispositions and life experiences.

The evolving self is a masterpiece in progress, a blend of the genetic canvas we are born with and the myriad strokes of experience and environment. Understanding the roles of nature and nurture in this journey helps in appreciating the complexity of human development. It underscores the beauty of our individuality, shaped by both the unchangeable code of our DNA and the ever-changing tapestry of our experiences. As we continue to evolve, we become more attuned to the intricate dance of nature and nurture, leading to a richer understanding and acceptance of ourselves and others.

Genetics and Personality:

The enigmatic journey of self-evolution is profoundly influenced by the intricate interplay of genetics (nature) and environmental factors (nurture), particularly in shaping personality. This narrative explores how these forces converge and diverge, casting light on the multifaceted process of personality development.

The Genetic Prelude: Nature's Imprint on Personality

Our story begins with genetics, which sets the stage for personality traits. Genetic inheritance provides a foundational framework for characteristics such as temperament, emotional reactivity, and perhaps even aspects of social behavior.

- **Temperamental Traits**: Traits like introversion/extroversion, emotional stability, and openness can have genetic underpinnings.

- **Hereditary Influences on Mood and Behavior**: Genetics can predispose individuals to certain mood patterns or behavioral tendencies, influencing their overall personality.

- **Inherited Resilience and Vulnerability**: Genetic factors can determine the resilience or susceptibility to stress and mental health challenges, shaping one's approach to life.

The Unfolding Canvas: Nurture's Role in Personality Development

While genetics lays the groundwork, it is nurture that often paints the intricate details of personality. Family upbringing, cultural milieu, educational experiences, and personal encounters all contribute to the evolution of one's character.

- **Family Dynamics**: Early familial interactions play a crucial role in forming attachment styles, self-esteem, and social attitudes.

- **Cultural and Social Influences**: The cultural context shapes values, beliefs, and norms, all of which feed into personality development.

- **Educational and Peer Interactions**: These experiences hone social skills, influence cognitive development, and contribute to one's sense of identity.

- **Life Events**: Significant personal experiences, whether traumatic or uplifting, can lead to profound shifts in personality traits.

Nature and Nurture: A Complex Interplay

The relationship between genetics and environmental influences in shaping personality is neither linear nor predictable but a dynamic interplay.

- **Gene-Environment Correlation**: People may seek out experiences that align with their genetic dispositions, creating a feedback loop where nature influences nurture choices.

- **Epigenetic Mechanisms**: Environmental factors can modify gene expression, leading to changes in personality traits without altering the underlying genetic code.

- **Adaptation and Change**: Individuals might develop traits or behaviors in response to their environment that seem at odds with their genetic predispositions.

Personality Evolution Through Life Stages

Personality is not static; it evolves through different life stages, influenced by changing environments and maturing genetic expressions.

- **Childhood and Adolescence**: This phase is critical for personality development, with significant plasticity in response to environmental inputs.

- **Adulthood**: In adulthood, there is often a stabilization of personality traits, yet significant life events or changes can still invoke shifts.

- **Later Years**: Older age often brings a re-evaluation of life experiences and can lead to further evolution of personality traits, sometimes highlighting genetic predispositions more prominently.

The evolving self, especially in the context of personality development, is a testament to the intricate dance of nature and nurture. Appreciating the influence of both genetics and environmental factors offers a richer understanding of personal growth and identity. This journey, marked by constant interaction between innate dispositions and life experiences, reveals the profound depth and adaptability of the human personality. As we navigate this journey, recognizing the roles of both nature and nurture not only helps in self-discovery but also fosters empathy and appreciation for the diverse tapestries of personality in others.

Environment and Experiences:

In the odyssey of self-evolution, the role of environment and experiences (nurture) alongside genetic predispositions (nature) is profoundly significant. This narrative delves into how environmental factors and personal experiences intertwine with genetic makeup to sculpt the journey of personal growth and identity formation.

Setting the Stage: The Genetic Foundation

The journey begins with our genetic endowment, a baseline from which individual development starts. These inherited traits provide the initial contours of our potential capabilities, predispositions, and vulnerabilities.

- **Inherited Traits**: These include a range of physical and psychological characteristics that set the stage for individual differences.

- **Genetic Predispositions**: These are tendencies towards certain behaviors, abilities, or health conditions, influenced by our genetic makeup.

Painting the Picture: The Role of Environment and Experiences

While genetics sets the stage, it is the environment and experiences that add depth and color to the canvas of self.

- **Family and Home Environment**: The family setting, parenting styles, and early life experiences play a crucial role in shaping personality, beliefs, and attitudes.

- **Cultural and Societal Context**: The broader cultural and social milieu influences values, norms, and worldviews, contributing significantly to personal development.

- **Educational Experiences**: Formal and informal education shapes cognitive abilities, social skills, and personal interests.

- **Life Events and Personal Experiences**: Significant events, both positive and challenging, have a profound impact on personal growth, resilience, and worldview.

The Dynamic Interplay of Nature and Nurture

The relationship between our genetic makeup and our experiences is not a simple cause-and-effect but a dynamic, ongoing interaction.

- **Gene-Environment Interaction**: Genetics can influence how individuals respond to their environment, and conversely, environmental factors can impact genetic expression.

- **Shaping and Reshaping of Traits**: While some traits are relatively stable, others are more malleable and can be shaped significantly by environmental factors and experiences.

- **The Role of Choice and Agency**: Individuals have the agency to shape their environment and experiences, which in turn influence their development.

Evolution Across the Lifespan

The journey of becoming is continuous, with different stages of life presenting unique interactions between nature and nurture.

- **Childhood and Adolescence**: This period is marked by rapid development, where environmental factors and experiences play a pivotal role in shaping identity.

- **Adulthood**: As individuals gain more control over their environment and choices, the influence of personal experiences becomes more pronounced.

- **Later Life**: Reflections on past experiences, combined with changes in environment and social roles, contribute to ongoing personal evolution.

The evolving self is a complex narrative of how genetic predispositions interact with the myriad of environmental factors and personal experiences. This journey highlights the fluidity of personal development, influenced by the ever-changing landscape of experiences and contexts. Understanding the roles of both nature and nurture in this process not only deepens self-awareness but also enhances our appreciation for the diverse paths of human development. As we continue to evolve, embracing the richness of our experiences and the nuances of our genetic makeup allows us to navigate the journey of becoming with greater insight and empathy.

PART II: STAGES OF EVOLUTION

Chapter 5: The Physical Self

The evolution of the self is an intricate journey that encompasses not just the mental and emotional facets of our being, but also the physical aspect. Understanding how our physical experiences shape and are shaped by our continuous journey of becoming offers profound insights into our overall personal development.

The Genesis: Physicality and Genetics

Our physical journey starts with the genetic blueprint we inherit. This genetic foundation dictates a range of physical characteristics and potentials.

- **Inherited Physical Traits**: These include height, bone structure, facial features, and other inherited physical attributes.

- **Genetic Health Dispositions**: Predispositions to certain physical conditions like allergies, heart disease, or athletic prowess are also part of this genetic inheritance.

- **Physical Development**: The pace and nature of physical growth during childhood and adolescence are largely governed by genetics.

Sculpting the Self: Physical Experiences and Environment

While genetics lay the foundation, our physical self is greatly molded by our experiences and environment.

- **Nutrition and Lifestyle**: Dietary habits and lifestyle choices significantly impact physical health, growth, and appearance.

- **Physical Activity and Training**: Engagement in physical activities and sports can dramatically alter the body's capabilities and appearance.

- **Environmental Interactions**: Exposure to different environmental factors, such as climate and pollution, also impacts physical development and health.

The Interplay of Nature and Nurture in Physical Self

The physical self is a testament to the dynamic interplay between our genetic endowment and our life experiences.

- **Physical Adaptations**: Our body adapts to the demands placed upon it, whether through exercise, diet, or environmental stressors.

- **Health and Well-being**: The interaction of genetic factors with lifestyle choices influences overall health and susceptibility to diseases.

- **Body Awareness and Image**: How we perceive and experience our physical selves is influenced both by our innate characteristics and our interactions with the environment.

Lifespan Evolution of the Physical Self

The physical aspect of the self evolves continually throughout the life cycle, responding to different stages of life, experiences, and environments.

- **Childhood and Adolescence**: This is a critical period for physical development, heavily influenced by nutrition, physical activity, and overall health.

- **Adulthood**: The physical self in adulthood is shaped by lifestyle choices, work environments, and physical activities.

- **Aging**: As we age, our physical self undergoes natural changes, influenced by lifelong habits, health practices, and genetic factors.

The evolution of our physical selves is a crucial part of our overall journey of becoming. It reflects not only our genetic heritage but also our interactions with the world around us. By understanding and embracing this aspect of self-evolution, we gain a fuller appreciation of how deeply intertwined our physical experiences are with our identity and personal growth. As we navigate through different phases of life, acknowledging the importance of nurturing our physical selves becomes essential to our holistic well-being and self-realization. The physical journey of becoming, with its unique challenges and triumphs, is a vital component of our human experience.

The Growing Body:

The journey of self-evolution is profoundly marked by the experiences of our growing body. From infancy through to old age, the physical transformations we undergo not only shape our identity but also influence our interactions with the world. This narrative explores the evolving self through the lens of the physical changes and challenges encountered at different stages of life.

The Dawn of Physical Being: Infancy and Childhood

The earliest stage of our physical journey is one of rapid growth and development.

- **Rapid Physical Growth**: Infants and children experience significant changes in size, strength, and coordination.

- **Motor Skill Development**: Learning to crawl, walk, and then run, children develop fine and gross motor skills essential for physical interaction with their environment.

- **Cognitive-Physical Interplay**: The development of physical abilities is closely tied to cognitive development, influencing how children learn and interact with their surroundings.

The Turbulent Seas of Adolescence

Adolescence marks a period of dramatic physical change, deeply intertwined with psychological and emotional transformations.

- **Puberty**: The onset of puberty brings about hormonal changes, leading to growth spurts, sexual maturation, and physical changes such as voice deepening in boys and breast development in girls.

- **Body Image and Self-Identity**: As their bodies change, adolescents grapple with body image issues, which can significantly impact their self-esteem and identity.

- **Increased Physical Capabilities**: With increased strength and endurance, adolescents explore new physical challenges and capabilities.

The Adult Body: Growth, Maintenance, and Adaptation

Adulthood is characterized by a stabilization in physical growth, with a focus on maintenance and adaptation.

- **Physical Peak and Plateau**: Early adulthood is often the physical peak, followed by a gradual plateau. Maintaining physical health and fitness becomes crucial.

- **Lifestyle Impacts**: Choices around diet, exercise, and lifestyle habits significantly affect physical health and capabilities.

- **Reproductive Phase**: For many, this period includes pregnancy and childbirth, which bring about profound physical and psychological changes.

The Mature Body: Embracing Change and Challenges

As we enter the later stages of life, our bodies undergo further changes.

- **Aging**: Aging is marked by a gradual decline in physical capabilities, changes in metabolism, and increased vulnerability to health issues.

- **Adapting to Limitations**: Adapting to physical limitations becomes a key aspect of self-evolution, requiring adjustments in lifestyle and activities.

- **Wisdom of the Body**: With age often comes a deeper understanding and acceptance of one's physical self, alongside a recognition of the importance of health and well-being.

The evolving physical self is a profound reflection of our journey through life. Each stage of physical development, from the helplessness of infancy to the strength of youth, and the wisdom of age, offers unique challenges and opportunities for growth. Our physical experiences shape not only how we view ourselves but also how we interact with the world around us. Embracing and understanding the changes in our physical being is integral to our overall personal evolution. This journey of the growing body, with its intricate connection to our mental, emotional, and spiritual selves, is a testament to the complex and beautiful process of becoming.

Aging Gracefully:

The evolution of the self is an ongoing narrative that gains profound depth and texture as we age. Aging gracefully is not just a concept of physical well-being, but a holistic integration of physical, emotional, and psychological growth. This narrative explores the journey of aging, focusing on how the physical self adapts and evolves, reflecting a life lived and the wisdom gained through years.

The Transition into Mature Adulthood

Aging is a natural progression, a testament to the life we have lived and the experiences we have gathered.

- **Physical Changes**: As we age, our bodies undergo natural changes – skin loses its elasticity, hair grays, and we may not be as physically agile as we once were.

- **Adapting to Change**: Acceptance and adaptation to these changes are crucial. It involves recognizing and respecting our body's evolving needs and limitations.

- **Health and Wellness Focus**: Prioritizing health through regular exercise, a balanced diet, and regular health check-ups becomes increasingly important.

The Middle Years: Embracing Change and Seeking Balance

The middle years of life are often a time of introspection and rebalancing, as physical changes become more evident.

- **Physical Activity and Maintenance**: Maintaining physical fitness through age-appropriate activities helps in managing health and preserving mobility.

- **Mind-Body Connection**: Practices like yoga, Tai Chi, or meditation can enhance the connection between mind and body, promoting holistic well-being.

- **Redefining Beauty and Strength**: This stage often involves redefining perceptions of beauty and strength, focusing more on wellness and vitality.

The Golden Years: Wisdom and Adaptation

As we move into our later years, our relationship with our physical selves continues to evolve.

- **Acceptance of Physical Changes**: There's an acceptance of the aging body, recognizing its journey and the experiences it has borne.

- **Cherishing Life Experiences**: Older adults often possess a rich tapestry of memories and experiences that shape their perspective on life and aging.

- **Adapting Lifestyles**: Adjustments in lifestyle to accommodate changing physical abilities are key. This might include modifying homes for better accessibility or engaging in gentler forms of exercise.

Psychological and Emotional Aspects of Aging

Aging gracefully is not solely a physical journey; it encompasses the psychological and emotional realms as well.

- **Emotional Resilience**: Many find increased emotional resilience and a capacity for deeper joy in simple pleasures.

- **Legacy and Continuity**: There's often a focus on legacy—what one wishes to leave behind, be it wisdom, memories, or life lessons.

- **Social Connections and Community**: Maintaining social connections and being part of a community can play a vital role in emotional well-being.

Conclusion

Aging gracefully is about embracing the journey of life with all its transformations. It's a process of honoring the wisdom of the body, acknowledging the beauty in its aging, and maintaining a harmonious balance between physical health and emotional well-being. This phase of life offers a unique perspective, colored by a rich tapestry of experiences, and is a crucial chapter in the continuous journey of becoming. As we navigate through our later years, we learn that aging is not just a physical process but a deeply personal and enriching experience, offering opportunities for growth, reflection, and joy.

Chapter 6: The Emotional Self

The self is a multidimensional process, where the emotional aspect plays a crucial role. The journey of our emotional self is about how we experience, understand, and express our feelings across different stages of life. This narrative delves into the continuous evolution of our emotional being, highlighting its impact on our overall personal growth and identity.

The Emergence of Emotional Awareness: Childhood and Adolescence

The foundation of our emotional journey is laid in the early years of life.

- **Emotional Development in Childhood**: Children begin to recognize and name emotions, learning to express feelings in a socially acceptable manner.

- **Family Influence**: The emotional environment at home, including how caregivers express and handle emotions, significantly shapes a child's emotional development.

- **Adolescence**: This stage introduces complex emotions and heightened emotional intensity, often accompanied by the struggle for emotional regulation and identity formation.

Young Adulthood: Emotional Exploration and Identity Formation

In young adulthood, emotional experiences become more nuanced and complex.

- **Emotional Intimacy and Relationships**: Forming deeper emotional bonds, including romantic relationships, becomes central, offering both challenges and growth opportunities.

- **Career and Aspirations**: Pursuing career goals and personal aspirations also brings a range of emotional experiences, from stress and anxiety to satisfaction and achievement.

- **Self-Discovery and Independence**: This period often involves exploring one's emotional self more deeply, leading to greater independence and self-awareness.

Midlife: Emotional Maturation and Reflection

Midlife often brings a shift in emotional perspective and priorities.

- **Re-evaluation and Introspection**: Many experience a re-evaluation of life choices and priorities, leading to significant emotional introspection.

- **Coping with Life Changes**: Dealing with changes such as aging, parenthood, and career transitions requires emotional adaptability and resilience.

- **Deepening Emotional Connections**: There's often a focus on deepening existing emotional connections and valuing quality over quantity in relationships.

Later Life: Wisdom and Emotional Integration

As individuals enter their later years, the emotional self tends toward integration and wisdom.

- **Emotional Regulation and Acceptance**: Older adults often exhibit better emotional regulation and acceptance, having navigated many emotional experiences.

- **Reflection and Legacy**: Reflecting on life's journey, focusing on legacy, and making sense of one's life story are common themes.

- **Coping with Loss and Change**: Managing loss, whether of loved ones, physical abilities, or independence, becomes a critical aspect of emotional health.

The Role of Challenges and Resilience

Throughout life, emotional challenges such as grief, trauma, and disappointment are inevitable.

- **Building Resilience**: Overcoming emotional challenges contributes to the development of resilience and emotional strength.

- **Learning from Experiences**: Each challenge presents an opportunity to learn and grow emotionally, enriching our understanding of ourselves and others.

The journey of the emotional self is an integral part of our overall evolution. It involves a continuous process of experiencing, understanding, and managing our emotions in ways that contribute to our personal growth and well-being. As we navigate through different life stages, our emotional experiences become richer and more complex, offering profound insights into who we are and our relationships with others. Embracing this emotional journey, with all its ups and downs, enables us to lead more fulfilling lives and to connect with others in meaningful ways. The evolving emotional self is not just about feeling, but about learning from our feelings to become more empathetic, resilient, and self-aware individuals.

The Emotional Roller Coaster of Adolescence:

The journey of the evolving self takes a particularly tumultuous turn during adolescence, a phase often marked by an emotional roller coaster. This critical period of transition is not just about physical growth but involves profound emotional upheaval and transformation. Understanding the emotional trajectory of adolescence is key to grasping how these formative years shape the evolving self.

The Onset of Adolescence: A Surge of Emotions

Adolescence is ushered in by a surge of hormonal changes, significantly impacting emotional states.

- **Hormonal Fluctuations**: These biological changes can cause mood swings, heightened emotional sensitivity, and unpredictability.

- **Self-Discovery and Identity Formation**: Adolescents embark on a quest for self-identity, often leading to intense emotions as they explore who they are and where they fit in the world.

Navigating Social Dynamics

Social interactions take on new dimensions and complexities during adolescence, deeply affecting emotional well-being.

- **Peer Influence and Belonging**: The desire to fit in with peers can evoke strong emotions, from the joy of acceptance to the distress of exclusion or bullying.

- **First Experiences of Romantic Love**: The exploration of romantic feelings introduces new emotional highs and lows, often coupled with the anxiety of navigating these uncharted territories.

The Struggle for Independence and Autonomy

The adolescent's journey is also marked by a struggle for independence, creating potential conflict and intense emotions.

- **Parent-Child Dynamics**: As adolescents push for more autonomy, this can lead to conflicts with parents, evoking feelings of frustration, anger, and sometimes alienation.

- **Decision Making and Consequences**: The process of making independent choices, along with dealing with their consequences, often elicits a wide range of emotions.

Emotional Vulnerability and Mental Health

Adolescence is a critical period for the emergence of mental health issues, often heightened by emotional vulnerability.

- **Mood Disorders and Anxiety**: Conditions such as depression and anxiety disorders may surface during these years, necessitating awareness and support.

- **Coping Mechanisms**: Adolescents develop unique coping mechanisms, some healthy and others potentially harmful, as they deal with emotional turmoil.

The Role of Environment and Support

The environment in which adolescents grow plays a crucial role in their emotional development.

- **Family Environment**: A supportive and understanding family environment can provide stability and a safe space for emotional expression.

- **School and Community**: Positive school experiences and community support systems can significantly buffer the emotional challenges of adolescence.

Maturation and Growth

Despite its challenges, adolescence is also a time of tremendous emotional growth and maturation.

- **Emotional Intelligence Development**: Adolescents learn to better understand and manage their emotions, contributing to emotional intelligence.

- **Resilience Building**: Navigating through emotional ups and downs, adolescents build resilience, preparing them for adult emotional experiences.

The emotional roller coaster of adolescence is a critical phase in the evolving self. It involves navigating a complex web of new emotions, social dynamics, and self-discovery. Understanding and supporting adolescents through this journey is crucial, as these years lay the groundwork for emotional maturity and identity formation. The emotional experiences of adolescence, with all their intensity and flux, are not just phases to endure but important steps in the lifelong journey of becoming. They shape the emotional landscape upon which the future self is built, imbued with resilience, empathy, and a deeper understanding of the human experience.

Maturing Emotions: From Reaction to Response:

The evolution of the emotional self is a fundamental aspect of human development, transitioning from impulsive reactions to thoughtful responses. This maturation of emotions is not merely a function of age but a complex process influenced by experiences, learning, and self-awareness. It's a journey from the often uncontrolled, instinctive reactions of youth to the more measured, reflective responses of maturity.

Childhood: The Realm of Instinctive Reactions

In early childhood, emotional expressions are primarily reactive and instinctual.

- **Immediate Emotional Reactions**: Children express emotions spontaneously, often unable to filter or moderate their feelings.

- **Learning Emotional Vocabulary**: As children grow, they start to learn the language to describe their emotions, which is the first step in understanding them.

- **Role of Caregivers**: Parents and caregivers play a crucial role in modeling emotional responses and teaching children about emotional regulation.

Adolescence: The Turbulent Transition

Adolescence is marked by intense emotional fluctuations, where reaction often overshadows response.

- **Hormonal Changes and Emotional Intensity**: The hormonal surges of adolescence can amplify emotional reactions, leading to mood swings and impulsive behavior.

- **Social and Peer Influences**: The desire for peer approval and fear of rejection can lead to reactive emotional behavior.

- **Developing Emotional Intelligence**: This stage is critical for developing self-awareness and empathy, skills essential for mature emotional responses.

Young Adulthood: The Path to Emotional Maturity

In young adulthood, the journey towards emotional maturity gains momentum.

- **Experience and Perspective**: Life experiences, including successes and failures, contribute to a broader perspective and a deeper understanding of emotions.

- **Self-Regulation Skills**: Young adults gradually learn to manage their emotions, shifting from immediate reactions to considered responses.

- **Relationships and Empathy**: Navigating complex relationships during this stage fosters empathy and the ability to respond to emotions in a nuanced manner.

Midlife: Reflection and Refinement

Midlife often brings a period of reflection, further refining emotional responses.

- **Re-evaluating Emotional Patterns**: Individuals may reassess long-held emotional patterns, understanding their roots and impacts.

- **Balance and Control**: There's often a greater balance between emotional impulses and rational thought, leading to more controlled responses.

- **Wisdom and Acceptance**: The wisdom gained through varied life experiences can lead to a more accepting and less reactive emotional stance.

Later Life: Mastery and Legacy

In later years, the culmination of a lifetime's emotional experiences results in a mastery of emotional responses.

- **Emotional Regulation and Resilience**: Older adults often show greater emotional regulation and resilience, having navigated diverse emotional landscapes.

- **Legacy of Emotional Wisdom**: Seniors can offer valuable emotional insights and guidance, drawn from their extensive life experiences.

- **Acceptance and Contentment**: There is often a sense of acceptance and contentment, as emotional responses are tempered by an understanding of life's transient nature.

The journey from reaction to response in our emotional lives is a continuous process of growth and learning. Each life stage contributes uniquely to this evolution, shaping how we perceive, experience, and respond to our emotions. This maturation is not just about controlling emotions but about understanding them, learning from them, and using them as guides for thoughtful action. As we evolve, our emotions become less about immediate reaction and more about informed response, reflecting the depth and richness of our life experiences. Embracing this journey enhances not only our personal well-being but also enriches our interactions with others, contributing to a more empathetic and understanding world.

Chapter 7: The Intellectual Self

The evolution of the self is an intricate tapestry woven from various threads, among which the intellectual self is paramount. This facet of our being, concerned with cognition, understanding, and knowledge, undergoes significant transformation throughout life. The intellectual journey is not merely about the accumulation of facts but involves developing critical thinking, problem-solving skills, and an ever-expanding worldview.

Early Childhood: The Foundations of Intellectual Curiosity

The intellectual journey begins in the wonder-filled years of early childhood.

- **Rapid Cognitive Development**: This phase is marked by a rapid expansion of cognitive abilities, including language acquisition, basic problem-solving, and understanding the world.

- **Curiosity and Exploration**: Children exhibit an innate curiosity, constantly exploring and questioning their environment, laying the groundwork for lifelong learning.

- **Role of Play**: Play is not just a source of amusement; it's a critical educational tool through which children learn and make sense of their world.

Adolescence: Intellectual Expansion and Identity Formation

Adolescence is a critical period for intellectual growth and identity formation.

- **Abstract Thinking**: This stage sees the development of abstract thinking, allowing teenagers to process complex concepts and engage in hypothetical reasoning.

- **Educational Challenges**: Formal education becomes more challenging, introducing advanced subjects and critical thinking skills.

- **Formation of Personal Beliefs and Values**: Adolescents begin to form their own beliefs and values, often questioning and evaluating the information received from authority figures and peers.

Young Adulthood: Intellectual Independence and Exploration

In young adulthood, intellectual development is characterized by greater independence and exploration.

- **Higher Education and Professional Training**: For many, this period involves tertiary education or specialized training, focusing on specific areas of interest or career paths.

- **Critical Analysis and Synthesis of Ideas**: Young adults learn to critically analyze information, synthesize diverse ideas, and develop informed opinions.

- **Application of Knowledge**: This is also a time for applying learned knowledge in real-world settings, whether in professional or personal contexts.

Midlife: Intellectual Maturation and Reflection

Midlife often brings a deeper level of intellectual maturation and reflective thought.

- **Life Experiences as a Learning Tool**: The wealth of personal and professional experiences becomes a source of learning and intellectual enrichment.

- **Re-evaluation of Beliefs and Knowledge**: Many individuals reassess previously held beliefs, leading to a more nuanced understanding of the world.

- **Continued Learning and Adaptability**: The pursuit of lifelong learning, whether through formal education or personal interests, remains vital.

Later Life: Wisdom and Intellectual Legacy

As individuals enter their later years, intellectual evolution often takes the form of wisdom.

- **Integration of Knowledge and Experience**: The vast reservoir of knowledge and life experiences integrates into a form of wisdom, offering a unique perspective on life.

- **Mentorship and Passing on Knowledge**: Older adults often take on mentorship roles, passing on knowledge and insights to younger generations.

- **Adapting to Cognitive Changes**: Navigating and adapting to age-related cognitive changes is also part of the intellectual journey in later life.

The intellectual self is not a static entity but a dynamic and evolving aspect of our being. From the exploratory learning of childhood to the reflective wisdom of old age, our intellectual journey is integral to our overall personal development. This continuous process of learning, questioning, and understanding not only enriches our own lives but also contributes to the collective knowledge and progress of society. Embracing the journey of the intellectual self means committing to a life of curiosity, open-mindedness, and continual growth, allowing us to fully engage with the ever-changing world around us.

The Quest for Knowledge:

The intellectual self is a fundamental component of our journey of becoming. This quest for knowledge is not just an accumulation of information but a deeper, transformative process that shapes our understanding of the world, our place in it, and our relationship with others. It involves a continual re-evaluation and expansion of our perspectives, driven by curiosity, critical thinking, and the desire to understand.

The Beginnings of Intellectual Curiosity: Childhood

The journey often begins in the wonder-filled years of childhood, where the seeds of intellectual curiosity are sown.

- **Innate Curiosity and Learning**: Children exhibit a natural curiosity, exploring their environment and incessantly asking questions to make sense of the world around them.

- **Foundation of Learning**: This stage sets the foundation for future intellectual pursuits, as children learn basic skills like reading, writing, and arithmetic, which are crucial for their academic journey.

- **Role of Play and Exploration**: Play is a significant aspect of learning, helping children develop problem-solving skills, creativity, and cognitive flexibility.

Adolescence: Expanding Horizons

As children transition into adolescence, their intellectual journey takes on new dimensions.

- **Development of Abstract Thinking**: Adolescents start to think abstractly and critically, beginning to challenge ideas and form their own opinions.

- **Educational Challenges**: This stage is marked by more rigorous academic demands, pushing adolescents to expand their knowledge base and intellectual skills.

- **Identity and Knowledge**: Intellectual development is closely tied to identity formation, as teenagers seek knowledge that resonates with their emerging sense of self.

Young Adulthood: Deepening Understanding

In young adulthood, the quest for knowledge often becomes more focused and purposeful.

- **Higher Education and Specialization**: Many delve into higher education or vocational training, specializing in areas of interest or career paths.

- **Critical Thinking and Analysis**: Young adults learn to critically assess information, synthesizing diverse perspectives to form well-rounded viewpoints.

- **Real-World Application**: This is a time for applying theoretical knowledge to practical challenges, whether in professional or personal life.

Midlife: Reflective Inquiry

Midlife often brings a phase of reflective inquiry and intellectual reassessment.

- **Life Experiences as a Source of Knowledge**: The wealth of personal and professional experiences becomes a rich source for learning and reflection.

- **Re-evaluation of Beliefs and Perspectives**: Many individuals reassess long-held beliefs and perspectives, leading to a more complex and nuanced understanding of the world.

- **Lifelong Learning**: The pursuit of lifelong learning, whether through formal education, self-study, or experiential learning, remains crucial.

Later Life: Integration and Wisdom

In later years, the intellectual journey often shifts towards integration and the sharing of wisdom.

- **Synthesis of Knowledge and Experience**: Decades of knowledge and experiences are synthesized into a form of wisdom, offering unique insights and perspectives.

- **Mentorship and Legacy**: Older adults frequently engage in sharing their knowledge, mentoring younger generations, and contributing to the collective wisdom of their communities.

- **Adaptation to Cognitive Changes**: Navigating cognitive changes with age is also a part of the intellectual journey, requiring adaptation and resilience.

The quest for knowledge is a lifelong odyssey that plays a crucial role in the evolving self. It is about constantly challenging our understanding, seeking new perspectives, and embracing the complexity of the world. This journey enriches not just our own lives but contributes to the collective growth of society. It demands openness, humility, and a relentless pursuit of understanding. In embracing this journey, we commit to a life of intellectual curiosity, growth, and the continuous redefinition of our understanding of the world and ourselves.

Wisdom Through the Ages:

The journey of the intellectual self, especially in the pursuit of wisdom, is a profound aspect of the human experience. It is a journey that stretches across the lifespan, transforming through various stages of life. Wisdom, distinct from mere knowledge, encompasses deep understanding, insight, and the ability to apply knowledge in practical, life-affirming ways. This narrative explores how wisdom is cultivated and expressed through different ages, contributing to the evolving self.

Childhood: The Seeds of Wisdom

The intellectual journey begins in childhood, where the foundation for future wisdom is laid.

- **Curiosity and Wonder**: Children approach the world with a sense of wonder and an insatiable curiosity, which are fundamental to the development of wisdom.

- **Learning from Experience**: Through play and exploration, children learn about cause and effect, empathy, and problem-solving, which are crucial components of wisdom.

- **Guidance from Elders**: The role of parents, teachers, and caregivers in modeling behavior and imparting early life lessons is instrumental in setting the groundwork for wise thinking.

Adolescence: The Formation of Insight

Adolescence is a critical period for the development of deeper insight and critical thinking.

- **Questioning and Exploration**: Teenagers begin to question established norms and beliefs, an essential process for the development of independent thought and wisdom.

- **Emotional Intelligence**: This stage is marked by the development of emotional intelligence, an integral part of wisdom that involves understanding and managing one's emotions and empathizing with others.

- **Cultural and Moral Understanding**: Exposure to diverse cultures and ethical discussions during these years helps in forming a more nuanced worldview.

Young Adulthood: The Refinement of Thought

In young adulthood, wisdom starts to take a more defined shape, influenced by broader experiences.

- **Higher Education and Learning**: For many, this stage involves higher education or acquiring specialized skills, contributing to cognitive development and critical thinking.

- **Life Experiences**: Real-world experiences, including successes and failures, relationships, and career challenges, provide fertile ground for developing practical wisdom.

- **Self-Reflection**: Young adults often engage in self-reflection, reassessing their values and beliefs, a process essential for the maturation of wisdom.

Midlife: Wisdom in Integration

Midlife often involves the integration of earlier life experiences and knowledge, leading to a deeper level of wisdom.

- **Synthesis of Knowledge and Experience**: The accumulation of life experiences, knowledge, successes, and setbacks is synthesized into a coherent understanding of life.

- **Empathy and Compassion**: Increased empathy and compassion for others, recognizing the complexity of human experiences, are hallmarks of wisdom at this stage.

- **Guidance and Mentorship**: Many in midlife find themselves in roles where they can guide and mentor others, applying their wisdom in practical, impactful ways.

Later Life: The Embodiment of Wisdom

In the later years of life, wisdom is often fully embodied and expressed.

- **Perspective and Acceptance**: Older adults tend to have a broad perspective on life, accepting its vicissitudes with equanimity and grace.

- **Legacy of Wisdom**: There's often a focus on passing down wisdom to younger generations, sharing life lessons, and contributing to the collective knowledge of the community.

- **Reflection and Transcendence**: Reflection on one's life journey contributes to a sense of transcendence, often leading to a profound understanding of life's deeper meanings.

Conclusion:

The journey of the intellectual self in the pursuit of wisdom is a continuous, evolving process. Each stage of life contributes uniquely to the development and expression of wisdom. This journey involves not only the accumulation of knowledge and experiences but also the cultivation of empathy, reflection, and a deep understanding of the human condition. Embracing this lifelong pursuit enriches not only the individual but also the wider community, fostering a deeper connection to the shared human experience. The evolving self, in its quest for wisdom, becomes a beacon of insight and understanding through the ages.

Chapter 8: The Spiritual Self

In the multifaceted journey of personal evolution, the spiritual self holds a unique and profound place. This aspect of our being is concerned with our sense of meaning, purpose, connection to something greater than ourselves, and the exploration of our inner consciousness. The spiritual journey is deeply personal and can vary greatly from one individual to another, yet it is a universal aspect of the human experience. It's about seeking answers to life's bigger questions and finding a sense of harmony within oneself and with the universe.

Childhood: The Dawning of Spiritual Awareness

In childhood, the seeds of spirituality are often sown, albeit in a formative and simplistic manner.

- **Innate Wonder and Awe**: Children naturally experience a sense of wonder and awe about the world, which can be seen as the roots of spirituality.

- **Early Religious and Cultural Influences**: For many, childhood spirituality is shaped by religious teachings and cultural traditions, providing a framework for understanding the world and their place in it.

- **Forming Basic Beliefs**: Children begin to form basic beliefs about life, morality, and the universe, influenced by their family, culture, and innate curiosity.

Adolescence: Questioning and Exploration

Adolescence is typically a time of questioning and exploring spiritual beliefs more deeply.

- **Challenging Established Beliefs**: Teenagers often challenge and question the religious and spiritual beliefs they have been taught, seeking their own truths.

- **Identity and Spirituality**: The formation of identity during this stage includes a spiritual dimension, as young people explore what they personally believe and value.

- **Exposure to Diverse Perspectives**: Increased exposure to different worldviews, cultures, and religions can expand adolescents' understanding of spirituality.

Young Adulthood: Deepening and Personalizing Spirituality

For many, young adulthood is a period of deeper exploration and personalization of their spiritual journey.

- **Seeking Meaning and Purpose**: Young adults often seek a deeper understanding of their purpose in life and how they connect to the larger world.

- **Integrating Spirituality into Life Choices**: Choices about career, relationships, and lifestyle may be influenced by one's spiritual beliefs and values.

- **Exploration of Different Spiritual Paths**: Some may explore various spiritual or philosophical systems, seeking a path that resonates with their personal experiences and beliefs.

Midlife: Reflection and Spiritual Maturation

Midlife often brings a period of reflection, reassessment, and maturation of one's spiritual beliefs.

- **Life Experiences as Spiritual Lessons**: The challenges and experiences of life can lead to a deeper spiritual understanding and often a re-evaluation of spiritual beliefs.

- **Seeking Harmony and Balance**: There's often a desire to find greater harmony and balance, both within oneself and in relation to the external world.

- **Transcendence and Legacy**: Thoughts may turn towards transcendence and the legacy one wishes to leave, which are deeply spiritual considerations.

Later Life: Integration and Wisdom

In later years, the spiritual journey often moves towards integration and wisdom.

- **Life Review and Spiritual Insights**: Reflecting on their life journey, many find deeper spiritual insights and a broader perspective on their personal experiences.

- **Sense of Connectedness**: There may be a heightened sense of connectedness with others, nature, or a higher power, and a focus on the essential, spiritual aspects of life.

- **Transmitting Spiritual Wisdom**: Older adults often serve as spiritual mentors or guides, passing on wisdom and insights to younger generations.

The spiritual aspect of the self is an ongoing and evolving journey that spans the course of a lifetime. It involves continually seeking, questioning, and deepening one's understanding of the profound questions of existence. This journey is not linear but often marked by periods of doubt, rediscovery, and new insights. Embracing the spiritual dimension of the self is about seeking harmony within and a deeper connection with the world around us. It's a quest that not only enriches our personal lives but also adds depth and meaning to our collective human experience. The evolving spiritual self, in its quest for understanding and connection, is a testament to the depth and complexity of what it means to be human.

Spirituality in Youth:

In the tapestry of personal development, the spiritual aspect during youth plays a pivotal role. This stage, often overshadowed by physical and intellectual growth, is crucial for laying the foundation of a person's spiritual identity. Youth is a time of exploration, questioning, and forming beliefs that can profoundly influence an individual's outlook on life, morality, and their sense of connection to something larger than themselves.

Early Encounters with Spirituality

In the early years, children's spirituality is often a reflection of their immediate environment, influenced by family, culture, and community.

- **Inherited Beliefs and Practices**: Many children adopt the religious and spiritual practices of their families, learning rituals, stories, and moral teachings.

- **Innate Wonder and Awe**: Children naturally experience a sense of wonder about the world, which is a fundamental aspect of spirituality. Their unfiltered curiosity and imagination often lend a spiritual quality to their exploration of life.

Adolescence: The Quest Begins

As children transition into adolescence, they begin to question and explore spirituality more consciously.

- **Questioning Established Beliefs**: This period is marked by a critical examination of inherited beliefs. Teenagers may challenge religious teachings or the absence of spiritual practices in their upbringing.

- **Identity and Belonging**: As adolescents struggle with questions of identity, spirituality can become a significant aspect of this exploration, helping them understand who they are and where they belong.

- **Exposure to Diversity**: Exposure to diverse spiritual and philosophical perspectives, whether through education, media, or peers, broadens their understanding and often prompts deeper personal reflection.

Young Adulthood: Deepening Understanding

In young adulthood, the exploration of spirituality often becomes more intentional and personal.

- **Personal Belief Systems**: Young adults begin to form their own belief systems, which may align with, modify, or completely differ from their childhood teachings.

- **Integration into Lifestyle**: Spirituality may influence choices regarding career, relationships, and lifestyle, reflecting the individual's values and beliefs.

- **Seeking Community and Connection**: There is often a search for like-minded individuals or communities that share similar spiritual values or are on a comparable quest for understanding.

Challenges and Opportunities

Youth is a period ripe with both challenges and opportunities for spiritual growth.

- **Crisis and Questioning**: Life challenges, such as personal loss or disappointment, can lead to profound spiritual questioning and sometimes a crisis of faith.

- **Moral and Ethical Development**: The development of a personal moral compass is closely tied to spiritual beliefs and is a significant aspect of youth.

- **Service and Altruism**: Engaging in service and altruistic activities, often motivated by spiritual values, can be a powerful means of spiritual expression and growth.

The Role of Mentors and Guides

The influence of mentors, be they parents, teachers, religious leaders, or other role models, is critical in shaping the spiritual aspect of youth.

- **Guidance and Support**: Positive role models can provide guidance, encourage questioning, and support in the exploration of spiritual beliefs.

- **Exemplifying Values**: The way these mentors live their beliefs can have a lasting impact, offering tangible examples of spirituality in action.

The spiritual journey during youth is a crucial part of the evolving self, marked by exploration, questioning, and the formation of a personal sense of spirituality. It involves navigating inherited beliefs, developing a personal moral framework, and seeking connection and meaning. This period lays the groundwork for a lifetime of spiritual growth, shaping how individuals view themselves, their place in the world, and their connection to a larger reality. Fostering a healthy spiritual development during youth involves encouraging exploration, providing support, and offering guidance, while respecting the individual's journey towards understanding and connection.

Evolving Beliefs and Finding Purpose:

The journey of the spiritual self, integral to the evolving nature of human existence, is often characterized by the evolution of beliefs and the pursuit of purpose. This narrative explores the trajectory of spiritual growth as individuals grapple with, refine, and often redefine their beliefs while seeking a deeper sense of purpose in their lives.

Childhood: The Foundation of Spiritual Beliefs

The journey begins in childhood, where initial beliefs are often shaped by family and cultural contexts.

- **Early Spiritual Learning**: Children absorb the religious and spiritual beliefs of their families, learning through stories, rituals, and observed practices.

- **Inherent Wonder and Curiosity**: The natural wonder and curiosity of children lead them to ask profound questions about life, existence, and the universe, setting the stage for future spiritual exploration.

Adolescence: Questioning and Exploration

Adolescence is a critical phase of questioning and exploration, where inherited beliefs are often scrutinized.

- **Challenging Established Beliefs**: Armed with a developing capacity for critical thinking, adolescents may question the beliefs they have been taught, seeking authenticity and personal relevance.

- **Formation of Individual Beliefs**: This period is marked by the formation of personal belief systems, which may or may not align with familial teachings.

- **Spiritual and Existential Questioning**: The search for identity during adolescence extends to spirituality, leading to deeper existential questions and the exploration of different philosophies and faiths.

Young Adulthood: Refining Beliefs and Seeking Purpose

In young adulthood, the refinement of spiritual beliefs and the search for purpose become more pronounced.

- **Integration of Spirituality**: As young adults establish their independence, they often integrate their spiritual beliefs into their life choices, from careers and relationships to lifestyle and social activism.

- **Expanding Spiritual Horizons**: Exposure to diverse perspectives, through education, travel, or interactions with a broader community, can lead to a more inclusive and nuanced spiritual outlook.

- **Purpose and Meaning**: The quest for purpose often intensifies, leading to questions about one's role in the world and the impact of one's actions.

Midlife: Deepening Understanding and Living Purpose

Midlife can bring a deeper understanding of spirituality and a more intentional living of one's purpose.

- **Reassessment and Deepening of Beliefs**: This stage often involves reassessing and deepening spiritual beliefs, sometimes triggered by life experiences such as loss, success, or failure.

- **Actualization of Purpose**: There's a shift towards actualizing one's purpose, whether through career changes, community involvement, or creative endeavors.

- **Transmitting Values and Wisdom**: Many in midlife take on roles of mentorship or leadership, transmitting their values and wisdom to others.

Later Life: Reflection and Legacy

In later years, spirituality often involves reflection on life and the legacy one leaves behind.

- **Integration and Wholeness**: The spiritual journey may move towards an integration of life experiences, leading to a sense of wholeness or fulfillment.

- **Contemplation of Mortality and Legacy**: Reflections on mortality and the kind of legacy to be left behind become central themes.

- **Sharing Wisdom and Insights**: Older adults often share their spiritual insights and wisdom, contributing to the spiritual growth of their communities and families.

Conclusion:

The evolving self, in its spiritual dimension, weaves a tapestry rich with evolving beliefs and the search for purpose. This journey is marked by continuous growth, reassessment, and deepening understanding. It is about finding meaning in life's experiences, contributing to the world in meaningful ways, and seeking connections that transcend the self. The spiritual journey, with its unique challenges and rewards, is integral to the overall narrative of becoming, adding depth, purpose, and richness to the human experience.

PART III: TOOLS FOR TRANSFORMATION

Chapter 9: Mindfulness and Meditation

The journey of the evolving self is deeply enriched by the practices of mindfulness and meditation. These disciplines, ancient yet ever-relevant, offer profound tools for personal growth and transformation. Mindfulness and meditation foster a heightened awareness of the present moment, a deeper understanding of our thoughts and emotions, and a greater sense of connection with ourselves and the world around us. This narrative explores how these practices influence and shape the journey of becoming.

The Beginnings: Discovering Mindfulness and Meditation

The introduction to mindfulness and meditation often begins as a response to the complexities and challenges of modern life.

- **Seeking Calm and Focus**: Many are drawn to these practices seeking relief from stress, anxiety, and the constant distractions of everyday life.

- **Initial Practices**: The journey typically starts with basic practices - focusing on breath, becoming aware of bodily sensations, and observing thoughts without judgment.

- **Early Benefits**: Practitioners often notice early benefits, including reduced stress, improved concentration, and a general sense of well-being.

Deepening the Practice: Integrating Mindfulness in Daily Life

As the practice deepens, mindfulness extends beyond formal meditation to become a part of daily life.

- **Moment-to-Moment Awareness**: Practitioners learn to maintain a mindful awareness throughout the day, in activities as mundane as eating, walking, or even in conversation.

- **Emotional Regulation and Awareness**: Through mindfulness, individuals become more attuned to their emotional states, learning to observe their reactions without being overwhelmed by them.

- **Cultivating Presence and Compassion**: Regular practice cultivates a presence that is fully engaged in the current moment, fostering a deeper empathy and compassion for others.

Meditation: Exploring Inner Landscapes

Meditation, as a more formal practice, takes the individual on a deeper exploration of their inner landscape.

- **Deep Relaxation and Insight**: Meditation allows for deep relaxation, providing space for insight and reflection.

- **Dealing with Mental Clutter**: It offers techniques to deal with the clutter of thoughts, helping to gain clarity and perspective.

- **Spiritual Connection**: For many, meditation becomes a spiritual journey, connecting them with a sense of something greater than themselves.

Challenges and Growth

The path of mindfulness and meditation is not without its challenges, yet these are integral to growth.

- **Facing Inner Challenges**: Practitioners often encounter internal resistance, old traumas, or deep-seated emotions, requiring courage and persistence to face.

- **Plateaus and Deepening Practice**: Plateaus in practice are common, inviting individuals to deepen their commitment or explore new meditation techniques.

- **Integrating Insights into Life**: One of the greatest challenges is integrating the insights gained from meditation into daily life, impacting relationships, work, and personal choices.

The Evolving Self: Transformation Through Mindfulness and Meditation

Over time, mindfulness and meditation can lead to profound transformations in the self.

- **Heightened Self-Awareness**: Regular practitioners often experience a heightened sense of self-awareness and a deeper understanding of their thought patterns and behaviors.

- **Altered Perspective on Life**: There's often a shift in how life is perceived - a greater appreciation for small moments, an increased sense of connection to others, and a deeper sense of purpose.

- **Resilience and Acceptance**: Mindfulness and meditation build resilience, helping individuals to accept life's challenges with equanimity and grace.

Mindfulness and meditation are not just practices but ways of being, offering tools to navigate the journey of life with greater awareness, compassion, and wisdom. This path is a continuous journey of becoming, where each moment is an opportunity for growth and understanding. As we evolve, these practices help to anchor us in the present, enriching our experience of life and deepening our connection to the world. The evolving self, nurtured by mindfulness and meditation, moves towards a state of balance, harmony, and profound understanding, reflecting the true potential of our human experience.

The Power of the Present Moment:

At the heart of the journey of the evolving self, particularly through mindfulness and meditation, lies the profound realization and embrace of the present moment. This narrative explores how the practice of being fully immersed in the 'now' is central to personal transformation and growth. Mindfulness and meditation do not just facilitate a deeper awareness of the present moment; they also unlock the potential within it, offering a path to a more fulfilling and balanced life.

Discovery of the Present Moment

The journey often begins with a simple yet profound realization – that life unfolds in the present moment.

- **Initial Encounters**: For many, their first encounter with mindfulness or meditation is through simple exercises focused on the breath or body sensations, grounding them in the immediacy of the now.

- **Shift from Autopilot to Awareness**: These practices help individuals shift from living on autopilot, with minds often lost in past memories or future worries, to a state of active awareness of the current moment.

Deepening Awareness Through Practice

As mindfulness and meditation practices deepen, so does the connection with the present moment.

- **Cultivating Mindfulness in Daily Activities**: Gradually, mindfulness extends beyond formal practice to everyday activities, turning routine actions into opportunities for awareness and presence.

- **Embracing the Full Spectrum of Experience**: Mindfulness encourages the acceptance of all aspects of the present moment – not just comfort and pleasure, but also discomfort, pain, and mundane experiences, thereby enriching the overall human experience.

Meditation and the Present Moment

In meditation, the present moment becomes a space for deeper exploration and understanding.

- **A Platform for Insight**: As the mind quietens, meditation offers a platform for insights into the nature of the self, thoughts, and emotions, often leading to a deeper understanding of personal patterns and behaviors.

- **Connection with Inner Self**: Regular meditation nurtures a connection with the inner self, fostering a sense of inner peace and equanimity that remains steady, irrespective of external circumstances.

Challenges and Growth

The path to embracing the present moment is replete with challenges, each offering opportunities for growth.

- **Overcoming Resistance**: Initially, there may be resistance – the mind may rebel against this stillness, highlighting the habitual patterns of escaping the present.

- **Learning from Difficulty**: Difficult emotions or thoughts that arise in the present are seen not as obstacles but as teachers, providing valuable lessons in self-awareness and resilience.

Transformative Impact of the Present Moment

Living in the present moment through mindfulness and meditation has a transformative impact on the evolving self.

- **Enhanced Clarity and Decision-Making**: With a mind anchored in the present, clarity and decision-making are enhanced, as actions are based on conscious awareness rather than automatic reactions.

- **Improved Emotional Well-being**: By not dwelling on the past or worrying about the future, individuals often find a significant improvement in their emotional well-being.

- **Cultivation of Gratitude and Joy**: There is an increased capacity for gratitude and joy, as even simple experiences are fully appreciated.

The Present Moment in Relationships and Connections

The power of the present moment extends beyond the individual to influence relationships and connections with others.

- **Deepened Relationships**: Being fully present in interactions with others leads to deeper and more meaningful connections.

- **Empathy and Compassion**: Mindfulness fosters empathy and compassion, as individuals become more attuned to the needs and feelings of others.

The journey of becoming, enriched by mindfulness and meditation, fundamentally revolves around the power of the present moment. This practice is not just an exercise in focus but a transformative experience that changes how we perceive ourselves, our lives, and our connections with others. It invites a richer, more vibrant engagement with life, where each moment is recognized as a precious opportunity for growth, learning, and connection. The evolving self, through the power of the present moment, discovers a path to greater peace, fulfillment, and harmony – a journey not just to a destination but an ongoing exploration of the depth and beauty of the immediate experience.

Meditation Techniques for Every Age:

The evolving self is greatly enhanced by the practice of mindfulness and meditation. These transformative practices offer tools that can be adapted to each stage of life, providing unique benefits suitable for the specific challenges and needs of every age. From the restless energy of childhood to the reflective pace of later years, meditation offers a pathway to deeper self-understanding, tranquility, and personal growth.

Childhood: Planting the Seeds of Mindfulness

In childhood, meditation techniques are tailored to engage a child's imagination and energy.

- **Short and Playful Practices**: Simple, brief practices that incorporate fun elements, like imagining a balloon expanding with each breath, are effective.

- **Guided Visualization**: Children respond well to guided visualizations that take them on imaginative journeys, promoting relaxation and creativity.

- **Mindful Movement**: Techniques like yoga or mindful walking, which combine physical activity with awareness, help children to connect with their bodies and the present moment.

Adolescence: Navigating Change with Mindfulness

For adolescents, meditation techniques can be geared towards managing emotions and coping with the changes and challenges of teenage years.

- **Breathing Exercises**: Techniques focusing on breath control can help manage anxiety and emotional swings, common in adolescence.

- **Body Scan Meditation**: This practice of paying attention to different parts of the body can promote relaxation and body awareness, important during the physical changes of puberty.

- **Mindful Journaling**: Encouraging teenagers to reflect and write about their daily experiences can be a form of mindful practice that helps them process their thoughts and emotions.

Young Adulthood: Building Focus and Clarity

In young adulthood, meditation can be a tool for enhancing focus, managing stress, and finding clarity in life's direction.

- **Concentration Meditation**: Practices that focus on a single point of reference, like the breath, a mantra, or a visual object, can enhance concentration and mental clarity.

- **Mindfulness-Based Stress Reduction (MBSR)**: This structured program combines mindfulness, meditation, and yoga to reduce stress and increase well-being.

- **Loving-Kindness Meditation**: This practice of cultivating compassion towards oneself and others can be especially beneficial for building relationships and empathy.

Midlife: Reflection and Mindful Awareness

Midlife meditation practices can focus on reflection, acceptance, and deepening self-awareness.

- **Insight Meditation (Vipassana)**: This practice encourages deep self-examination and mindfulness of thoughts, emotions, and sensations.

- **Zen Meditation**: Zen practices emphasizing simplicity and the cultivation of presence can be particularly helpful for those seeking a deeper understanding of life.

- **Walking Meditation**: This form of meditation combines mindful walking with contemplation, suitable for those who find peace in gentle movement.

Later Life: Embracing Tranquility and Wisdom

In later years, meditation can focus on embracing tranquility, letting go, and connecting with a sense of wisdom.

- **Guided Relaxation and Visualization**: Techniques that promote relaxation and visualization can help in coping with physical discomfort or pain and promote a sense of peace.

- **Gratitude Meditation**: Focusing on gratitude can enhance well-being, bringing a sense of fulfillment and contentment.

- **Mindful Reflection**: Practices that involve reflecting on life experiences can provide a sense of integration, wisdom, and closure.

Conclusion:

Throughout the evolving self's journey, mindfulness and meditation serve as constant companions, adaptable to the unique needs and capabilities of each life stage. These practices offer invaluable tools for personal growth, emotional regulation, and spiritual exploration. Whether it's through playful visualization in childhood, focused breathing in adolescence, or reflective practices in the later years, meditation enriches every stage of life. It provides a pathway not just to peace and calm but to a deeper understanding of oneself and a richer engagement with the world. The journey of becoming, supported by the timeless art of meditation, is one of continuous discovery, growth, and transformation.

Chapter 10: Therapy and Counseling

The evolving self is often marked by periods of introspection, challenge, and growth. Therapy and counseling play a pivotal role in this journey, offering a space for understanding, healing, and transformation. As individuals navigate various stages of their lives, therapy can provide support and guidance, helping them to unravel complex emotions, overcome obstacles, and achieve personal growth.

Early Life: Laying the Foundations

In childhood and adolescence, therapy can be instrumental in addressing developmental challenges and laying a healthy foundation for future growth.

- **Childhood Therapy**: Focuses on issues like behavioral problems, family dynamics, and coping with school-related stress. Play therapy is commonly used, allowing children to express themselves in a safe and supportive environment.

- **Adolescent Counseling**: Addresses issues unique to teenagers such as identity formation, peer pressure, and emotional regulation. Counseling at this stage often involves helping adolescents navigate their emerging independence while developing healthy coping strategies.

Young Adulthood: Navigating Change and Identity

As individuals enter young adulthood, therapy often centers on navigating life transitions and solidifying a sense of self.

- **Navigating Transitions**: Major life changes like starting college, beginning a career, or entering relationships can be focal points for therapy.

- **Identity and Self-Understanding**: Counseling can help young adults understand and accept their identities, including aspects related to sexuality, beliefs, and personal values.

- **Mental Health Management**: Issues like anxiety, depression, or the onset of other mental health conditions often emerge during this time, and therapy provides tools and strategies for management and healing.

Midlife: Reflection and Reassessment

Therapy during midlife often involves reflecting on past experiences and reassessing life goals and values.

- **Midlife Transition and Crisis**: Individuals may seek therapy to navigate the challenges of midlife, such as career dissatisfaction, aging, or changing family dynamics.

- **Re-evaluating Life Choices**: Therapy can provide a space to reflect on past decisions, reassess life goals, and make meaningful changes.

- **Coping with Loss or Illness**: This period may involve dealing with loss, whether it be the death of loved ones, health issues, or other forms of loss and grief.

Later Life: Integration and Acceptance

In later years, therapy often focuses on integrating life experiences, dealing with aging, and finding acceptance.

- **Life Review and Acceptance**: Therapy can assist in processing a life review, helping individuals find meaning and acceptance in their life journey.

- **Coping with Physical Changes**: Addressing the challenges of aging, including health issues and loss of independence, can be a significant part of counseling.

- **Legacy and End-of-Life Issues**: Discussions around legacy, end-of-life decisions, and coping with bereavement are important therapeutic themes in later life.

Throughout Life: Support and Growth

Regardless of the life stage, therapy offers continuous support and opportunities for personal growth.

- **Mental Health Maintenance**: Just as one might regularly visit a doctor for physical health, ongoing therapy can maintain and improve mental health.

- **Relationship and Communication Skills**: Therapy can enhance interpersonal skills, improving relationships with family, friends, and colleagues.

- **Crisis Management and Resilience Building**: Counseling provides support in times of crisis and helps build resilience to face future challenges.

Therapy and counseling are invaluable tools in the journey of the evolving self. By offering a safe space for exploration, healing, and understanding, therapy supports individuals through the complexities of each life stage. It aids in unraveling and processing emotions, confronting challenges, and fostering personal growth and self-awareness. As a companion in the journey of becoming, therapy enriches the human experience, guiding individuals towards a more integrated, fulfilled, and authentic existence.

When to Seek Help:

The self-evolution is a complex and multi-layered process, often requiring external support to navigate its many challenges. Therapy and counseling are vital tools that can guide individuals through various stages of their life, offering clarity, support, and healing. Understanding when to seek help is crucial in this journey, as timely intervention can significantly enhance personal growth and wellbeing.

Recognizing the Need for Help

The decision to seek therapy or counseling often arises from a recognition of personal struggles or challenges that seem insurmountable alone.

- **Emotional Distress**: Persistent feelings of sadness, anxiety, anger, or emotional numbness can be indicators that professional help is needed.

- **Life Transitions**: Major life changes, such as starting a new job, going through a divorce, or dealing with loss, can trigger emotional responses that warrant professional support.

- **Interpersonal Difficulties**: Consistent problems in relationships, whether with family, friends, or colleagues, may suggest underlying issues that could be explored in therapy.

Early Stages: Prevention and Growth

Seeking help in the early stages of distress can prevent more severe problems later on.

- **Preventive Measures**: Therapy can be a preventive measure, providing tools and strategies to manage stress and cope with life's challenges effectively.

- **Personal Development**: Counseling can also be pursued for personal development, such as improving communication skills, increasing self-awareness, or working on self-esteem issues.

During Crises: Navigating Turbulence

Therapy is particularly crucial during times of crisis, providing support and guidance to navigate turbulent periods.

- **Crisis Intervention**: In moments of acute distress, such as during a mental health crisis or after a traumatic event, immediate therapeutic intervention is essential.

- **Navigating Grief and Loss**: Therapy can be a supportive space to process grief and loss, helping individuals to find ways to cope and adjust to their new reality.

Chronic Conditions: Ongoing Support

For chronic mental health conditions, ongoing therapy is often necessary for management and quality of life.

- **Managing Chronic Mental Health Issues**: Conditions like depression, anxiety disorders, bipolar disorder, and others often require regular counseling for effective management.

- **Long-Term Support**: Long-term therapy provides a consistent support system, helping individuals understand their conditions and develop coping mechanisms.

Reflective and Later Stages: Seeking Meaning and Closure

In reflective periods of life or later stages, therapy can assist in finding meaning, acceptance, and closure.

- **Reflective Life Review**: Therapy can help individuals in reflecting on their life, understanding past events, and making peace with them.

- **End-of-Life Concerns**: For older adults, counseling can address fears and concerns about aging, loneliness, and end-of-life issues.

Recognizing when to seek therapy or counseling is a critical step in the journey of the evolving self. It's about understanding that seeking help is not a sign of weakness but a courageous step towards self-care and growth. Therapy can be a powerful resource at any life stage, offering support, insight, and tools for managing life's complexities. By embracing therapy as a valuable resource, individuals can navigate their personal journeys more effectively, leading to enhanced wellbeing and a more fulfilling life journey.

The Therapeutic Relationship as a Catalyst for Change:

In the evolving journey of self, therapy and counseling stand out as powerful catalysts for personal growth and transformation. Central to this transformative process is the therapeutic relationship – a unique and dynamic bond between therapist and client that is built on trust, empathy, and collaboration. This narrative delves into how the therapeutic relationship acts as a cornerstone for meaningful change and self-discovery.

The Foundation of the Therapeutic Relationship

The therapeutic relationship is the bedrock upon which the process of personal growth and healing is built.

- **Trust and Safety**: The foundation of this relationship is trust and a sense of safety, allowing clients to open up and explore difficult aspects of their lives.

- **Empathy and Understanding**: Therapists provide a non-judgmental, empathetic presence that validates the client's experiences and emotions.

- **Collaboration**: This relationship is collaborative; both therapist and client work together to set goals, explore issues, and devise strategies for change.

Navigating the Self through Connection

The therapeutic relationship provides a mirror for self-exploration and understanding.

- **Self-Reflection**: In the presence of a compassionate therapist, clients can explore their thoughts, feelings, and behaviors more deeply and honestly.

- **Insight and Awareness**: The therapist's feedback and perspective offer clients new insights into their patterns, contributing to increased self-awareness.

- **Corrective Emotional Experiences**: The therapeutic relationship can offer corrective emotional experiences, especially for those with past relational traumas, helping to reshape expectations and behaviors in relationships.

Facilitating Change and Growth

The dynamics of the therapeutic relationship are instrumental in facilitating personal change and growth.

- **Challenging and Supportive**: Therapists challenge clients' unhealthy patterns while providing support and encouragement, creating a balance that fosters growth.

- **Modeling Healthy Interactions**: Therapists often model healthy communication and boundary-setting, which clients can internalize and apply in their own lives.

- **Empowerment**: Through this relationship, clients are empowered to take control of their lives, make positive changes, and develop resilience.

The Role of Empathy and Validation

Empathy and validation within the therapeutic relationship are crucial for healing and self-acceptance.

- **Feeling Understood**: When clients feel understood and accepted, they are more likely to be open and engaged in the therapeutic process.

- **Normalization of Experiences**: Therapists help clients understand that their feelings and experiences are valid, normalizing them and reducing feelings of isolation or shame.

Transformation through Relationship

The therapeutic relationship itself can be a direct agent of transformation.

- **Relational Healing**: For clients with relational wounds, the therapeutic relationship can be a healing experience, providing a safe space to explore and understand these wounds.

- **Transference and Countertransference**: The phenomena of transference and countertransference can be used therapeutically to understand and work through unresolved issues.

Conclusion:

The therapeutic relationship is a journey of co-creation, where therapist and client work together to foster growth, healing, and self-discovery. It is a unique and dynamic bond that not only supports but actively propels individuals in their journey of becoming. Through empathy, collaboration, and mutual respect, this relationship becomes a powerful catalyst for change, offering a safe harbor for exploration and a launching pad for personal transformation. In the evolving self's journey, the therapeutic relationship is more than a mere component of therapy; it is a profound connection that can illuminate the path to a more authentic and fulfilling life.

Chapter 11: Physical Practices for Mental Growth

The evolving self is not solely a mental or emotional endeavor; it deeply intertwines with the physical domain. Physical practices, ranging from exercise to mindful movement, play a significant role in fostering mental growth and emotional well-being. This narrative explores how physical activities contribute to the development and enrichment of the mind, aiding in the continuous journey of becoming.

The Interconnection of Mind and Body

The foundational principle in this journey is the recognition of the intricate connection between the mind and body.

- **Holistic Well-being**: Physical health and mental health are profoundly interconnected, with each influencing and reinforcing the other.

- **Neurological Impact**: Physical activities can have a direct impact on brain health, influencing mood, cognitive function, and stress levels.

Exercise and Mental Growth

Regular physical exercise is a powerful tool for mental and emotional development.

- **Stress Reduction**: Exercise is known to reduce levels of the body's stress hormones, such as adrenaline and cortisol, and stimulate the production of endorphins, the body's natural mood elevators.

- **Cognitive Clarity and Focus**: Engaging in physical activities, especially those requiring coordination and strategy, can enhance cognitive functions like concentration, memory, and problem-solving skills.

- **Emotional Resilience**: Regular exercise can build emotional resilience, equipping individuals to better handle stress and adversity.

Mindful Movement Practices

Mindful movement practices, such as yoga and tai chi, offer a more integrated approach to mental and physical well-being.

d-Body Harmony: These practices focus on the alignment of body and mind, encouraging a of presence and awareness.

agement and Relaxation**: Techniques involving controlled breathing and mindful
re effective in managing stress and inducing relaxation.

ess and Emotional Regulation: Engaging in mindful movement enhances self-
nd emotional regulation, key components of mental growth.

The Role of Physical Challenges

Physical challenges, such as endurance sports or learning a new physical skill, can significantly contribute to mental growth.

- **Building Resilience and Confidence**: Overcoming physical challenges builds resilience, boosts confidence, and fosters a sense of accomplishment.

- **Learning from Failure**: Physical activities often involve trial and error, teaching valuable lessons about persistence, learning from failure, and the importance of continuous effort.

Nature and Mental Well-being

Engagement with nature through physical activities can have a profound impact on mental health.

- **Nature as a Healer**: Activities like hiking, gardening, or simply spending time in natural settings can reduce anxiety, improve mood, and enhance a sense of well-being.

- **Sensory Engagement**: Nature engages the senses in a unique way, providing a refreshing break from the overstimulation of modern life.

Rest and Recovery

Physical practices for mental growth also encompass the critical aspect of rest and recovery.

- **Restorative Practices**: Practices such as restorative yoga or relaxation techniques are crucial for mental health, providing the body and mind time to rejuvenate.

- **Sleep and Mental Health**: Adequate and quality sleep is a vital physical practice, directly impacting cognitive function, mood, and overall mental health.

The evolving self's journey encompasses a harmonious integration of physical practices for mental growth. Recognizing and utilizing the symbiotic relationship between physical activity and mental well-being is essential for holistic personal development. From the adrenaline rush of intense physical exercise to the calming flow of mindful movements, these practices are vital components in the continuous journey of becoming. They foster resilience, clarity, and emotional balance, paving the way for a more fulfilled and self-aware existence.

Yoga, Tai Chi, and Movement:

In the pursuit of personal growth and mental wellness, the integration of physical practices like yoga, Tai Chi, and mindful movement is essential. These disciplines, rooted in ancient traditions, offer more than just physical benefits; they are profound tools for mental and emotional growth. They bridge the gap between body and mind, facilitating a journey of holistic self-evolution.

Yoga: Unity of Body and Mind

Yoga, an ancient practice with deep spiritual roots, offers a comprehensive approach to mental growth.

- **Mind-Body Harmony**: Yoga's combination of postures (asanas), breathing techniques (pranayama), and meditation promotes a harmonious balance between body and mind.

- **Stress Reduction and Emotional Release**: Regular yoga practice is known to decrease stress and anxiety, helping in the release of emotional blockages.

- **Enhanced Self-awareness**: Yoga cultivates heightened self-awareness, encouraging practitioners to observe their mental and emotional states with clarity and mindfulness.

Tai Chi: The Moving Meditation

Tai Chi, often described as meditation in motion, is a gentle practice that emphasizes fluidity, balance, and calm.

- **Flow and Mindfulness**: The slow, deliberate movements of Tai Chi keep the practitioner grounded in the present moment, enhancing mindfulness.

- **Stress Management**: Its meditative aspect helps in managing stress and anxiety, promoting a state of mental calm and clarity.

- **Balance and Coordination**: Tai Chi improves physical balance and coordination, which in turn can positively affect mental and emotional stability.

Mindful Movement: Attuning to the Present

Mindful movement practices involve moving the body with full awareness, connecting with the present moment.

- **Awareness in Action**: These practices teach individuals to pay attention to their body's movements, breath, and alignment, fostering a deep sense of presence.

- **Physical and Mental Integration**: By focusing on the connection between movement and breath, practitioners can achieve a state of mental tranquility and emotional balance.

- **Variety and Accessibility**: Mindful movement can be incorporated into various activities, such as walking, dancing, or simple daily tasks, making it accessible to all.

The Role of Breathing

In all these practices, the role of controlled and conscious breathing is paramount.

- **Regulating the Nervous System**: Proper breathing techniques help regulate the nervous system, reducing stress and promoting relaxation.

- **Emotional Balance**: Breath control can be a powerful tool for managing emotions, helping practitioners stay calm and centered in challenging situations.

Mental Growth and Physical Discipline

These physical practices contribute to mental growth by instilling discipline, perseverance, and resilience.

- **Discipline and Focus**: Regular practice requires discipline and focus, traits that are transferable to other areas of life, enhancing overall mental strength.

- **Coping with Discomfort**: Learning to navigate physical discomfort in these practices can build mental and emotional resilience.

- **Body Awareness and Mental Health**: Increased body awareness leads to better recognition of stress and anxiety symptoms, allowing for earlier intervention and management.

Incorporating yoga, Tai Chi, and mindful movement into the journey of self-evolution offers a holistic path to personal growth. These practices blend physical discipline with mental and emotional introspection, leading to a profound understanding and connection with oneself. They teach the art of presence, balance, and harmony, essential components for mental growth and a fulfilling journey of becoming. As individuals engage in these practices, they embark on a transformative journey that nurtures the mind, body, and spirit in unison, leading to a more balanced, aware, and enriched life.

The Mind-Body Connection:

The personal evolution is deeply rooted in the synergy between the mind and the body. Understanding and harnessing this mind-body connection through physical practices is a powerful catalyst for mental growth and self-discovery. This narrative explores how physical activities, when mindfully engaged, can significantly contribute to the evolving self, enhancing cognitive functions, emotional well-being, and overall life satisfaction.

The Foundations of the Mind-Body Connection

The mind-body connection is a fundamental concept that acknowledges the intricate interplay between physical health and mental well-being.

- **Biological Interactions**: Psychological states can affect physical health, and bodily conditions can influence mental states. This bidirectional relationship is mediated through pathways like the nervous system, hormones, and immune response.

- **Holistic Perspective**: A holistic approach to health and personal development recognizes that caring for the body is inherently caring for the mind, and vice versa.

Physical Exercise and Cognitive Enhancement

Engaging in physical exercise is not just about improving physical fitness but also about enhancing cognitive abilities.

- **Neurogenesis and Brain Health**: Regular physical activity promotes neurogenesis (the formation of new neurons) and increases brain-derived neurotrophic factor (BDNF), crucial for brain health and cognitive functions.

- **Improved Concentration and Memory**: Exercises, especially those requiring coordination and strategy, improve concentration, memory, and executive functions.

- **Mood Regulation**: Physical activity stimulates the release of endorphins and serotonin, which play a vital role in mood regulation and the reduction of stress and anxiety.

Mindful Movement Practices: Yoga and Tai Chi

Mindful movement practices like yoga and Tai Chi are exemplary in strengthening the mind-body connection.

- **Mindfulness and Presence**: These practices encourage mindfulness, the act of being fully present and engaged in the moment, which enhances mental clarity and focus.

- **Emotional Balance**: The combination of movement, breath, and attention provides a unique way to manage and balance emotions, fostering a sense of inner calm and resilience.

- **Body Awareness**: Developing a heightened awareness of bodily sensations and movements enhances the understanding of the body's signals, often leading to better emotional and psychological insights.

The Role of Breathwork

Breathwork is a key component in many physical practices, serving as a bridge between the mind and the body.

- **Regulating the Nervous System**: Controlled breathing techniques can activate the parasympathetic nervous system, inducing a state of calm and relaxation.

- **Emotional Release and Healing**: Conscious breathing can be a tool for releasing emotional blockages, facilitating healing and emotional well-being.

Integrating Physical Activity into Daily Life

Incorporating physical practices into daily routines can continuously nurture the mind-body connection.

- **Routine Activities**: Simple activities like walking, stretching, or any form of gentle movement can be performed mindfully to reap mental benefits.

- **Work-Life Balance**: Integrating physical practices in daily life helps in maintaining work-life balance, reducing burnout, and enhancing productivity.

Challenges and Adaptation

Embracing physical practices for mental growth involves facing and adapting to personal challenges.

- **Overcoming Physical Limitations**: Learning to work with and adapt to physical limitations or disabilities in these practices can be a profound experience of personal growth and acceptance.

- **Resilience and Perseverance**: Physical challenges teach resilience, perseverance, and the ability to face and overcome obstacles, which are essential qualities for mental and emotional strength.

Conclusion:

The journey of becoming, through the lens of the mind-body connection, is a harmonious and integrative path. Physical practices for mental growth are not just exercises for the body but nourishment for the mind and soul. They foster a deeper understanding of oneself, enhance cognitive and emotional faculties, and contribute significantly to overall life satisfaction and fulfillment. In recognizing and nurturing this connection, individuals can unlock new dimensions of their evolving selves, leading to a more balanced, aware, and enriched existence.

Chapter 12: Journaling and Reflective Practices

In the intricate process of self-evolution, journaling and reflective practices stand out as powerful tools for personal growth and self-awareness. These practices involve introspection and self-examination, enabling individuals to explore their thoughts, emotions, and experiences. This narrative explores how journaling and other reflective practices contribute to the evolving journey of the self, aiding in understanding one's inner world and fostering personal development.

The Art of Journaling

Journaling is more than just a method of recording daily events; it's a pathway to deeper self-understanding and clarity.

- **Self-Expression and Emotional Release**: Writing in a journal provides a safe space for expressing thoughts and emotions, often leading to emotional release and healing.

- **Clarity and Understanding**: Regular journaling helps in untangling complex thoughts, providing clarity and insight into personal issues and challenges.

- **Tracking Progress and Growth**: Keeping a journal allows individuals to track their personal growth over time, observing patterns, changes, and milestones in their journey.

Reflective Practices

Reflective practices encompass a range of activities that encourage deep thinking and introspection.

- **Meditative Reflection**: Practices such as meditation can be combined with reflection, creating a quiet space to ponder life's experiences and one's reactions to them.

- **Mindful Contemplation**: Mindfulness, the practice of being present in the moment, can be a form of reflection that fosters a deeper understanding of one's thoughts and feelings in the here and now.

The Benefits of Writing and Reflection

Engaging in journaling and reflective practices offers numerous benefits for mental and emotional well-being.

- **Stress Reduction**: Writing about stressful experiences can help in managing and reducing stress.

- **Problem-Solving and Creativity**: These practices encourage creative thinking and can provide new perspectives on problems, facilitating more effective problem-solving strategies.

- **Enhanced Self-Esteem**: By exploring and affirming personal experiences and feelings, these practices can lead to enhanced self-esteem and a stronger sense of identity.

Integrating Journaling into Everyday Life

Making journaling and reflection a part of daily life can maximize their benefits.

- **Routine Practice**: Setting aside a regular time for journaling and reflection can make them a valuable part of one's daily routine.

- **Different Formats and Approaches**: People may find different formats (like bullet journaling, digital journaling, or audio recording) more suitable depending on their lifestyle and preferences.

- **Combining with Other Activities**: Journaling can be combined with other activities like reading, walking, or after meditation for added insight.

Challenges and Mindful Approach

While journaling and reflective practices are beneficial, they also come with challenges that require a mindful approach.

- **Dealing with Uncomfortable Insights**: Reflection can sometimes bring up uncomfortable truths or memories; approaching these with self-compassion and patience is crucial.

- **Maintaining Consistency**: Keeping up with regular journaling or reflection can be challenging; it's important to find a rhythm that works for each individual without feeling pressured.

Journaling and reflective practices are invaluable components in the journey of becoming. They offer unique pathways to self-discovery, allowing individuals to explore the depths of their inner selves, articulate their experiences, and gain insights into their personal journeys. These practices not only enhance self-awareness but also contribute to emotional health and personal development. By regularly engaging in these practices, individuals can foster a deeper connection with themselves, navigate life's complexities with greater clarity, and continue on their path of self-evolution with enhanced understanding and purpose.

Writing for Insight:

In personal evolution, journaling and reflective writing stand as powerful tools for gaining insight and understanding. This form of self-expression not only chronicles the journey but also unravels the complex tapestry of thoughts, emotions, and experiences. Writing for insight is a practice that encourages introspection, fosters self-awareness, and aids in navigating the path of self-development.

The Role of Journaling in Self-Discovery

Journaling serves as a mirror, reflecting the inner workings of the mind and soul.

- **Capturing Inner Thoughts and Feelings**: Writing helps in articulating thoughts and emotions that might otherwise remain unexamined or misunderstood.

- **Patterns and Trends**: Over time, journal entries can reveal patterns in thoughts and behaviors, offering valuable insights into personal habits, triggers, and preferences.

- **Processing Experiences**: Reflective writing provides a means to process and make sense of life experiences, both positive and negative.

Techniques for Insightful Journaling

There are various approaches to journaling that can enhance self-insight and personal growth.

- **Free Writing**: Writing without inhibition or structure can unlock deeper thoughts and emotions, allowing for unfiltered expression.

- **Prompted Writing**: Using specific prompts or questions can guide the writing process, providing focus and direction for reflection.

- **Gratitude Journaling**: Regularly noting things one is grateful for can shift focus to positive aspects of life, enhancing overall well-being.

The Therapeutic Benefits of Writing

Journaling is more than a practice of self-expression; it has therapeutic benefits that impact mental and emotional health.

- **Stress Relief**: The act of writing can be a stress-relief tool, helping to calm the mind and release pent-up emotions.

- **Enhanced Emotional Intelligence**: Regularly exploring and writing about emotions can lead to a better understanding of them, enhancing emotional intelligence.

- **Problem-Solving**: Writing about challenges can help in breaking them down and finding effective solutions.

Reflective Practices Beyond Writing

While journaling is a key component, other reflective practices also contribute to self-insight.

- **Meditative Reflection**: Combining journaling with meditation can deepen the reflective experience, allowing for a more profound connection with the inner self.

- **Dialogue Writing**: Writing imagined dialogues with different parts of oneself or with significant others can offer new perspectives and deeper understanding.

- **Artistic Expression**: For some, combining writing with visual arts like drawing or painting can be a powerful way to express and understand complex emotions.

Overcoming Challenges in Journaling

While beneficial, journaling and reflective practices can also present challenges.

- **Facing Uncomfortable Truths**: Writing can unearth uncomfortable emotions or memories; it's important to approach these with self-compassion.

- **Maintaining Consistency**: Developing a regular journaling habit requires discipline; it's important to find a rhythm that feels natural and sustainable.

Journaling and reflective practices are invaluable companions in the journey of becoming. They serve as tools for introspection, self-expression, and emotional catharsis. Through the practice of writing for insight, individuals can explore the depths of their psyche, understand their evolving selves better, and navigate the complexities of life with greater clarity and purpose. Embracing journaling as a habitual practice opens up pathways to personal growth, emotional resilience, and a deeper understanding of one's journey through life.

Other Reflective Modalities: Art, Music, and Dance:

The path of self-evolution is enriched not only through words and written reflection but also through various other modalities like art, music, and dance. These creative practices offer unique avenues for self-expression, introspection, and communication with the deeper aspects of the self. They can be powerful tools in the journey of personal growth, providing insight, healing, and a deeper connection with one's inner world.

Art: A Canvas for Self-Exploration

Art, in its many forms, serves as a potent medium for reflection and self-discovery.

- **Visual Expression**: Painting, drawing, and sculpting allow for the expression of emotions and thoughts that might be difficult to articulate verbally.

- **Therapeutic Benefits**: Engaging in artistic activities can be therapeutic, offering a sense of calm, focus, and a way to process complex feelings.

- **Symbolism and Metaphor**: Art enables the exploration of personal experiences through symbolism and metaphor, providing insights into subconscious thoughts and feelings.

Music: The Rhythm of the Soul

Music, both in listening and creation, is a powerful tool for emotional exploration and expression.

- **Emotional Resonance**: Music can evoke and help process a wide range of emotions, from joy to sorrow, offering a cathartic experience.

- **Creating and Composing**: Writing music or lyrics allows for a deeply personal form of expression, capturing the nuances of one's inner experiences.

- **Music Therapy**: Participating in music therapy sessions can aid in managing stress, improving mood, and fostering emotional well-being.

Dance: Movement as a Language

Dance offers a dynamic way to connect with and express the evolving self.

- **Embodied Expression**: Dance uses the body as a medium of expression, enabling individuals to communicate feelings and stories through movement.

- **Mind-Body Connection**: It strengthens the mind-body connection, promoting physical health, emotional release, and mental clarity.

- **Cultural and Personal Narratives**: Different styles of dance can reflect cultural narratives as well as personal stories, contributing to a sense of identity and belonging.

Integrating Creative Modalities into Reflective Practice

Incorporating these creative modalities into regular reflective practice can enhance the journey of self-evolution.

- **Regular Practice**: Just like journaling, regular engagement in artistic, musical, or dance activities can deepen their impact on personal growth.

- **Combining Modalities**: These practices can be combined – for instance, painting or dancing to music, or writing about an art or dance experience, to enrich the reflective process.

- **Mindful Engagement**: Approaching these activities mindfully, focusing on the process rather than the end product, can enhance their therapeutic value.

Challenges and Personalization

Engaging with art, music, and dance for reflection and growth also comes with its unique challenges and considerations.

- **Overcoming Self-Judgment**: It's important to engage in these activities without self-criticism or judgment, focusing on the process of creation and reflection.

- **Finding Personal Resonance**: Individuals should explore different forms of creative expression to find what resonates most deeply with them and their unique journey.

Conclusion:

Art, music, and dance, along with journaling and other reflective practices, create a symphony of modalities for self-discovery and personal evolution. These creative avenues open up new ways of understanding and connecting with the self, allowing for a richer, more nuanced exploration of personal experiences and emotions. They offer alternative languages for the soul, facilitating a deeper dialogue within and fostering a journey of continuous growth and transformation. In the evolving self's quest for understanding and expression, these modalities stand as powerful allies, each offering its unique melody in the orchestra of personal development.

PART IV: NAVIGATING CHALLENGES

Chapter 13: Stagnation and Plateaus

In self-evolution, periods of stagnation and plateaus are as integral as the phases of growth and breakthrough. These moments, often perceived negatively, are crucial in the overarching process of personal development. Understanding and navigating through these periods of apparent standstill can lead to deeper insights and renewed momentum in the journey of becoming.

The Nature of Stagnation and Plateaus

Stagnation and plateaus can manifest in various aspects of personal growth, be it emotional, intellectual, spiritual, or physical.

- **Emotional Stagnation**: This may present as a lack of emotional growth, where one feels stuck in the same patterns of reacting and relating.

- **Intellectual Plateaus**: Here, one might experience a lack of inspiration or motivation to learn and engage intellectually, feeling as if their knowledge or skills are not advancing.

- **Spiritual Stagnation**: This could involve a sense of disconnection or lack of progression in one's spiritual practices and beliefs.

- **Physical Plateaus**: In physical fitness or health, this refers to a period where there is no noticeable improvement or change despite consistent effort.

The Significance of Stagnation and Plateaus

These periods serve important functions in the journey of self-evolution.

- **Time for Integration**: Plateaus can provide necessary time for the integration of new insights, skills, or changes that have been recently developed.

- **Reflection and Reassessment**: Stagnation often prompts reflection, allowing one to reassess their goals, methods, and motivations.

- **Rest and Recovery**: These phases can also be a natural time for rest and recovery, which is essential for long-term growth and well-being.

Navigating Through Stagnation and Plateaus

Approaching these periods constructively can turn them into valuable experiences.

- **Mindful Acceptance**: Accepting the plateau or period of stagnation without judgment can be the first step in moving through it.

- **Seeking New Perspectives**: Sometimes, seeking external input, like reading new material, talking to mentors, or engaging in different experiences, can provide fresh perspectives and ideas.

- **Adjusting Goals and Methods**: It may be necessary to adjust one's goals, approach, or techniques. Sometimes, subtle changes can reignite progress.

Learning from Stagnation and Plateaus

These periods offer unique learning opportunities.

- **Understanding Personal Rhythms**: They teach about personal rhythms and cycles in growth, underscoring that development is not always linear.

- **Developing Resilience**: Navigating through these phases develops resilience and the ability to handle future challenges more effectively.

- **Enhancing Self-Awareness**: They often lead to increased self-awareness, as one explores the reasons behind the stagnation or plateau.

Embracing Stagnation and Plateaus as Part of Growth

Ultimately, embracing these periods as natural and essential parts of the journey is crucial.

- **Recognizing Growth in Stillness**: Sometimes, the most significant growth happens in stillness or when progress is not outwardly visible.

- **Valuing the Process**: Understanding that the journey of self-evolution is as much about the process as it is about the outcome can transform one's perspective on stagnation and plateaus.

In the continuous journey of becoming, stagnation and plateaus are not merely obstacles but vital phases that contribute to the depth and richness of personal growth. They invite introspection, adaptation, and resilience, playing a critical role in the complex process of self-evolution. By embracing and navigating through these periods with awareness and patience, they can become powerful catalysts for renewed growth and deeper understanding, marking another significant stride in the evolving journey of the self.

Identifying the Rut:

In the personal growth, encountering periods of stagnation or hitting a plateau – often referred to colloquially as being 'in a rut' – is an inevitable and natural phase. Recognizing and acknowledging these periods is crucial in the evolving journey of the self. This narrative delves into how one can identify when they are in a rut and understand its implications in the broader context of personal development.

Characteristics of Being in a Rut

Stagnation or hitting a plateau manifests in various forms, often subtly creeping into our daily routines and mental states.

- **Lack of Progress**: A clear sign of being in a rut is the feeling that you're not making progress despite your efforts, especially in areas where you previously experienced growth.

- **Diminished Enthusiasm**: A loss of interest or enthusiasm in activities that once excited or challenged you can indicate that you're in a rut.

- **Routine Monotony**: Life feels monotonous and routine, lacking in variety or excitement, and you might feel like you're just going through the motions.

Emotional and Psychological Indicators

Emotional and psychological signs are often the first indicators of being in a rut.

- **Persistent Frustration or Discontent**: Feelings of frustration, discontent, or unexplained sadness can be symptomatic of stagnation.

- **Mental Fatigue or Burnout**: A sense of mental fatigue, apathy, or burnout, even when you're not physically exerting yourself, can signal a deeper issue of stagnation.

- **Feeling Stuck or Helpless**: Persistent feelings of being stuck or an inability to envision a way forward are hallmark signs of being in a rut.

Impact on Personal Growth

Being in a rut has a significant impact on the journey of self-evolution.

- **Impeded Growth**: Personal growth feels impeded, as if you've hit an invisible barrier that's preventing further development.

- **Questioning Self-Worth**: These periods can lead to self-doubt and questioning of one's abilities and worth, especially if identity is closely tied to progress and achievement.

Causes of Stagnation and Plateaus

Identifying the underlying causes of being in a rut is critical to addressing it effectively.

- **External Factors**: Changes in life circumstances, such as a job change, relocation, or relationship issues, can contribute to feelings of stagnation.

- **Internal Factors**: Internal factors, such as fear of failure, comfort in the status quo, or lack of clear goals, can also lead to a plateau.

- **Overexertion and Lack of Rest**: Sometimes, continuous exertion without adequate rest and recovery can lead to burnout, manifesting as a rut.

Navigating Out of the Rut

Recognizing that you are in a rut is the first step towards moving out of it.

- **Seeking New Challenges**: Engaging in new activities or learning new skills can provide a fresh perspective and reinvigorate your enthusiasm.

- **Mindfulness and Reflection**: Practicing mindfulness and reflecting on your current state can help you understand your emotions and the reasons behind your feelings of stagnation.

- **Setting Small, Achievable Goals**: Breaking down larger goals into smaller, manageable tasks can create a sense of accomplishment and forward momentum.

Identifying and understanding periods of stagnation or being in a rut is a crucial aspect of the evolving self. These phases, while challenging, are an integral part of the journey of personal growth. They offer opportunities for introspection, realignment, and rediscovery of purpose and passion. Embracing these periods, rather than resisting them, can lead to deeper self-awareness, renewed motivation, and ultimately, continued personal evolution. The journey of becoming is not always linear, and these plateaus are essential landscapes in the rich topography of self-development.

Breaking Free and Moving Forward:

In the dynamic process of self-evolution, encountering periods of stagnation and hitting plateaus is an inevitable experience. While these phases may seem like obstacles, they are, in fact, integral to the journey, offering critical opportunities for introspection and recalibration. Breaking free from these periods and moving forward is a vital aspect of personal growth, and understanding how to navigate these phases is crucial for the evolving self.

Understanding Stagnation and Plateaus

Recognizing the signs of stagnation and plateaus is the first step in overcoming them.

- **Recognizing the Signs**: Symptoms such as a lack of enthusiasm, feeling stuck, or a decrease in productivity can indicate that you're in a rut.

- **Assessing the Causes**: Identifying whether internal factors (like fear or loss of motivation) or external circumstances (like changes in environment) are contributing to the stagnation is key.

Strategies for Breaking Free

There are several strategies that can be employed to break free from periods of stagnation and move forward.

- **Setting New Goals**: Revisiting and setting new, achievable goals can provide a renewed sense of direction and purpose.

- **Changing Routines**: Altering daily routines, trying new activities, or changing your environment can stimulate different parts of your brain and reignite your creativity.

- **Seeking Inspiration**: Engaging with inspiring content, people, or experiences can provide fresh perspectives and ideas.

The Role of Self-Reflection

Self-reflection is a powerful tool in understanding and moving past stagnation.

- **Reflective Practices**: Engaging in practices like journaling, meditation, or mindfulness can offer insights into why you're feeling stuck and how to address it.

- **Learning from the Past**: Reflecting on how past challenges were overcome can provide strategies and reassurance that current plateaus can also be navigated successfully.

Seeking External Support

Sometimes, external support can be instrumental in moving past periods of stagnation.

- **Professional Guidance**: Seeking the help of a therapist, coach, or mentor can provide professional guidance and support.

- **Community and Relationships**: Leaning on your support network for encouragement and advice can be extremely beneficial.

Embracing and Learning from the Plateau

Viewing stagnation and plateaus as opportunities for growth rather than setbacks is essential.

- **Embracing the Process**: Understanding that growth is not always linear and that these phases are a natural part of the process can help in accepting and embracing them.

- **Learning and Growing**: Each plateau offers unique lessons; identifying and learning from these can lead to personal growth and development.

Implementing Small Changes for Big Impacts

Small, incremental changes can often lead to significant progress.

- **Small Steps**: Implementing small changes in habits or routines can lead to significant improvements over time.

- **Celebrating Small Wins**: Recognizing and celebrating small achievements can boost morale and motivation.

Maintaining Momentum

Once you've started to move past a period of stagnation, maintaining momentum is important.

- **Consistent Effort**: Continuously applying effort, even in small ways, can help maintain progress.

- **Regular Check-ins**: Regularly assessing your goals and progress can help keep you on track.

Conclusion:

The journey of the evolving self is characterized by ebbs and flows, with periods of rapid growth as well as times of stagnation and plateaus. Understanding and effectively navigating these phases are crucial for continuous personal development. By embracing these periods, utilizing reflective practices, seeking support, and implementing changes, individuals can break free from stagnation and continue on their path of growth and self-discovery. Each phase, whether of progression or plateau, offers valuable lessons and opportunities for development, contributing to the rich and ever-evolving tapestry of the self.

Chapter 14: External Influences and Peer Pressures

The self-evolution is not an isolated process; it unfolds within a complex network of social interactions and external influences. Peer pressure and the influence of societal norms play a significant role in shaping an individual's journey. This narrative delves into how external influences and peer pressures intersect with the evolving self, impacting the journey of personal growth and identity formation.

Understanding External Influences

External influences include the myriad societal, cultural, and social factors that impact an individual's thoughts, behaviors, and choices.

- **Cultural and Societal Norms**: These are the unwritten rules and expectations set by the society and culture one lives in, which can dictate acceptable behavior, lifestyle choices, and values.

- **Media and Social Media**: In the digital age, media and social media platforms are potent forces shaping perceptions, ideals, and aspirations.

- **Family and Community**: The values, beliefs, and expectations of one's family and immediate community also significantly influence personal development.

The Dynamics of Peer Pressure

Peer pressure is a specific type of external influence where individuals feel compelled to conform to the expectations or behaviors of their peers.

- **Conformity and Belonging**: The human need for belonging can lead to conformity, where individuals adjust their behaviors and beliefs to align with their peer group.

- **Positive vs. Negative Peer Pressure**: Peer pressure can be both positive (encouraging healthy behavior) and negative (promoting harmful or against one's own values).

- **Impact on Decision-Making**: Peer influence can significantly impact critical areas of decision-making, including career choices, relationships, and lifestyle habits.

The Evolving Self in the Context of External Pressures

Navigating external influences and peer pressures is a crucial aspect of personal evolution.

- **Identity Formation**: During adolescence and young adulthood, external influences are particularly impactful in shaping one's identity and self-concept.

- **Self-Awareness and Autonomy**: Developing self-awareness and autonomy is key in discerning which external influences align with one's true self and values.

- **Resilience and Critical Thinking**: Building resilience against negative influences and fostering critical thinking are essential skills in this journey.

Strategies to Navigate External Influences

Dealing with external pressures involves developing strategies to maintain personal integrity and authenticity.

- **Setting Boundaries**: Learning to set healthy boundaries with peers and external influences is crucial for self-preservation and growth.

- **Seeking Diverse Perspectives**: Exposing oneself to diverse perspectives and experiences can help in forming a well-rounded, independent viewpoint.

- **Self-Reflection and Core Values**: Regular self-reflection helps in staying connected with one's core values, serving as a guide in the midst of external pressures.

The Role of Support Systems

A strong support system plays a vital role in navigating the journey of becoming amidst external influences.

- **Positive Role Models and Mentors**: Having role models or mentors who exemplify healthy autonomy and self-respect can be influential.

- **Community and Belonging**: Finding a community that shares similar values and encourages positive growth can counteract negative peer pressures.

In the evolving self's journey, external influences and peer pressures are both challenges and catalysts for growth. Balancing these influences requires self-awareness, critical thinking, and resilience. It involves discerning which influences to embrace and which to resist, making choices that align with one's authentic self. By navigating these external pressures skillfully, individuals can forge their unique path of personal growth, enriched by the external world yet rooted in their true self and values. This balance is a dynamic and continuous process, integral to the evolving narrative of the self.

Societal Expectations:

In the odyssey of self-evolution, societal expectations represent a formidable external influence, shaping beliefs, behaviors, and life choices. These expectations, often ingrained and subtle, exert a profound impact on the journey of personal development. This narrative explores how societal norms and expectations interact with the evolving self, influencing identity formation, decision-making, and personal growth.

The Weight of Societal Expectations

Societal expectations encompass the often unspoken rules and standards set by the broader culture and community.

- **Cultural Norms and Roles**: These are the traditional roles and norms prescribed by culture, dictating acceptable behaviors and lifestyles, which can vary greatly across different societies.

- **Professional and Academic Standards**: Expectations regarding career success, educational attainment, and financial stability are major societal pressures that can define one's sense of worth and success.

- **Relationship and Family Dynamics**: Societal norms often dictate expectations around family life, marriage, and relationships, influencing personal choices in these areas.

Impact on the Evolving Self

Societal expectations can both constrain and guide the evolving self.

- **Identity and Self-Perception**: Conforming to societal expectations can sometimes lead to a conflict between one's true self and the self that society approves of.

- **Decision-Making**: Choices regarding career, education, relationships, and lifestyle are often heavily influenced by societal standards and expectations.

- **Stress and Mental Health**: The pressure to conform to these societal norms can lead to increased stress, anxiety, and in some cases, depression.

Navigating Societal Expectations

Developing strategies to navigate societal expectations is crucial for maintaining authenticity and personal well-being.

- **Critical Thinking**: Questioning and critically evaluating societal norms allows for a more conscious and autonomous approach to life choices.

- **Self-Awareness**: Being aware of one's values, desires, and beliefs helps in distinguishing between what is personally important and what is externally imposed.

- **Assertiveness and Boundaries**: Learning to assertively communicate one's choices and set boundaries can be vital in resisting undue societal pressure.

The Role of Peer Influence

Peers can both reinforce and challenge societal expectations, playing a significant role in the evolving self's journey.

- **Reinforcement of Norms**: Peer groups often reinforce societal norms, either explicitly through advice and comments or implicitly through their behaviors and choices.

- **Challenging and Reshaping Norms**: Conversely, peers can also provide a space to challenge and reshape societal norms, especially when they share similar values of authenticity and individuality.

Embracing Individuality amidst Societal Expectations

Balancing societal expectations with personal authenticity is a key aspect of self-evolution.

- **Personal Values vs. Societal Norms**: Aligning decisions with personal values, even when they conflict with societal expectations, is crucial for authentic living.

- **Seeking Supportive Environments**: Finding communities and networks that support individuality and personal growth can counterbalance the pressure of societal norms.

The journey of the evolving self is marked by a dynamic interplay between personal authenticity and societal expectations. Navigating this landscape requires self-awareness, resilience, and the courage to uphold personal values and choices. While societal norms can provide a framework and sense of belonging, true personal growth and fulfillment often lie in charting a course that resonates deeply with one's own beliefs and aspirations. Embracing this journey allows for a life lived not just by societal standards but enriched with personal meaning and authenticity.

Finding Your Authentic Path:

In the multifaceted journey of self-evolution, one of the most profound challenges is navigating the myriad of external influences and peer pressures while staying true to one's authentic path. The evolving self is constantly interacting with, and often shaped by, the expectations and norms of society, the influence of peers, and the omnipresent cultural narratives. This narrative explores how individuals can acknowledge these external forces and yet carve out a path that is authentically their own.

The Labyrinth of External Influences

The journey begins in a labyrinth where every turn presents new external influences and pressures.

- **Social and Cultural Conditioning**: From early life, individuals are conditioned by their social and cultural environment, which shapes their beliefs, values, and perceptions.

- **Peer Influence**: Friends and social circles exert significant influence, often dictating trends, behaviors, and life choices.

- **Media and Public Opinion**: The media, in its various forms, can significantly sway opinions and create societal pressures to conform to certain standards or ideals.

Recognizing External Pressures

The first step in finding an authentic path is recognizing these external pressures and their impact.

- **Self-Reflection**: Regular self-reflection helps in identifying areas where external influences are at odds with personal values or desires.

- **Awareness of Dissonance**: Feeling a sense of dissonance or discomfort can be an indicator that external pressures are misaligned with one's true self.

The Challenge of Peer Pressure

Peer pressure can be both overt and subtle, influencing decisions in ways that may not align with one's true preferences or aspirations.

- **Conformity vs. Individuality**: The desire to fit in or be accepted can often lead to conformity, overshadowing individual preferences and desires.

- **Critical Assessment of Relationships**: Evaluating relationships and social interactions to discern whether they support or hinder personal authenticity is crucial.

Cultivating Authenticity

Developing a strong sense of self and cultivating authenticity involves both introspection and action.

- **Defining Personal Values and Beliefs**: Identifying and articulating personal values and beliefs is foundational in setting the course for an authentic path.

- **Aligning Actions with Values**: Consistently aligning choices and actions with these personal values reinforces a sense of authenticity.

Resisting External Pressures

Resisting external pressures requires strength, resilience, and often, a deliberate strategy.

- **Building Resilience**: Developing emotional and mental resilience helps in standing firm against societal pressures and expectations.

- **Selective Influence**: Being selective about the influences one allows into their life, such as choosing positive and supportive relationships, is key.

Embracing One's Unique Journey

Every individual's journey is unique, and embracing this uniqueness is vital to finding an authentic path.

- **Celebrating Individuality**: Recognizing and celebrating one's unique qualities and experiences fosters a stronger sense of self.

- **Learning from Diverse Experiences**: Being open to diverse experiences and perspectives can enrich one's understanding of themselves and their path.

Conclusion:

The continuous journey of becoming, amidst external influences and peer pressures, is an ongoing navigation towards authenticity. It involves recognizing and understanding external pressures, aligning with personal values, and resisting conformity when it conflicts with one's true self. By embracing individuality and cultivating an authentic path, individuals can experience a deeper sense of fulfillment and purpose. This journey is not about rejecting external influences outright but about discerning which influences align with and enrich one's own journey of self-evolution.

Chapter 15: Dealing with Loss and Trauma

In the landscape of personal evolution, dealing with loss and trauma is an inevitable yet profoundly challenging part of the journey. These experiences, often marked by intense pain and upheaval, can fundamentally change an individual's perspective and path of growth. This narrative explores how facing loss and trauma is integral to the evolving self, contributing to a deeper understanding of resilience, strength, and the human spirit.

The Impact of Loss and Trauma

Loss and trauma can manifest in many forms, each leaving a distinct imprint on the individual's psyche and life journey.

- **Emotional and Psychological Impact**: Experiencing loss or trauma often results in a complex array of emotions, including grief, anger, confusion, and despair.

- **Reevaluation of Self and Life**: These experiences can lead to a profound reevaluation of one's beliefs, values, and understanding of the world.

- **Changes in Identity**: In the wake of trauma or loss, individuals often grapple with changes in their sense of identity and purpose.

Navigating the Initial Aftermath

The initial aftermath of loss or trauma is often the most turbulent period, requiring coping strategies and support.

- **Seeking Support**: Reaching out to friends, family, support groups, or mental health professionals can provide essential guidance and comfort.

- **Allowing Grief and Emotion**: Allowing oneself to fully experience and express grief is crucial for healing. Suppressing emotions can lead to longer-term complications.

- **Self-Care**: Engaging in self-care practices, such as rest, nutrition, and gentle physical activity, is essential to maintain physical and emotional health during this time.

The Process of Healing

Healing from loss and trauma is not a linear process but involves navigating through various stages and emotions.

- **Acknowledgment and Acceptance**: Recognizing and accepting the reality of the loss or trauma is a significant step in the healing process.

- **Processing Emotions**: Engaging in activities like journaling, art, or therapy can help process the complex emotions associated with these experiences.

- **Finding Meaning**: Many find healing in discovering or creating meaning from their experiences, whether through personal growth, helping others, or spiritual understanding.

Resilience and Personal Growth

In the long term, dealing with loss and trauma can contribute to a strengthened sense of resilience and personal growth.

- **Building Resilience**: Navigating through these challenges can build resilience, equipping individuals with the strength to handle future adversities.

- **New Perspectives and Empathy**: These experiences often lead to a deeper understanding of life, greater empathy for others, and a renewed appreciation for meaningful moments.

- **Transformative Change**: For some, these experiences act as catalysts for significant life changes or a reorientation of priorities and values.

Incorporating Loss and Trauma into the Self

Integrating the experiences of loss and trauma into one's life narrative is a critical aspect of the evolving self.

- **Identity Integration**: Recognizing that these experiences are a part of one's story, but not the entirety of it, helps in building a multifaceted identity.

- **Continued Connection**: Finding ways to maintain a sense of connection to what or whom was lost, while continuing to move forward, can be a comforting aspect of adaptation.

Dealing with loss and trauma is an inextricable part of the journey of becoming. These experiences, though deeply painful, are also rich with the potential for personal growth, resilience, and profound understanding of the complexities of life. The evolving self, through navigating the tumultuous waters of grief and trauma, can emerge with a deeper sense of compassion, strength, and a renewed purpose. Embracing these experiences as integral to one's personal evolution is not only an act of survival but one of courageous growth and transformation.

Grief as Transformation:

The journey of self-evolution is profoundly affected by the experience of loss and trauma, with grief acting as a pivotal point of transformation. Grief, while inherently painful and challenging, can also be a powerful catalyst for personal growth and change. This narrative delves into how the experience of grief, as a response to loss and trauma, can be an integral part of the evolving self, leading to deep transformation.

The Landscape of Grief

Grief is a complex, multifaceted response to loss, encompassing a wide range of emotions and experiences.

- **Emotional Spectrum of Grief**: It involves a spectrum of emotions, from sadness and anger to guilt and loneliness, often experienced in unpredictable waves.

- **Physical and Psychological Impact**: Grief can also manifest physically, affecting sleep, appetite, and energy levels, and can lead to psychological challenges such as anxiety and depression.

The Process of Grieving

Grieving is not a linear process but a journey with its unique rhythm and timeline for each individual.

- **Stages of Grief**: While traditionally conceptualized in stages, modern understanding recognizes that grief is more fluid, with individuals moving through different emotions in no set order.

- **Personal and Unique Experience**: Each person's experience of grief is unique, influenced by their relationship to what was lost, their support systems, and their personal coping mechanisms.

Transformation Through Grief

In the midst of its challenges, grief has the potential to be transformative.

- **Self-Discovery and Resilience**: Navigating through grief often leads to a deeper understanding of oneself, uncovering strengths and resilience that may not have been apparent before.

- **Reevaluation of Life**: The finality of loss can prompt individuals to reevaluate their lives, priorities, and values, often leading to significant life changes.

- **Increased Empathy and Compassion**: Experiencing profound loss can increase one's capacity for empathy and compassion, both for oneself and for others.

Navigating Grief in the Journey of Becoming

Integrating the experience of grief into the journey of becoming involves several key approaches.

- **Allowing and Acknowledging Grief**: Giving oneself permission to grieve fully and acknowledging the pain is crucial for healing.

- **Seeking Support**: Engaging with supportive friends, family, or professional counselors can provide comfort and guidance.

- **Finding Expression for Grief**: Finding ways to express grief, whether through writing, art, or other forms of expression, can be therapeutic.

The Role of Rituals and Remembrance

Rituals and acts of remembrance can play a significant role in the grieving process.

- **Creating Rituals**: Engaging in personal or cultural rituals can provide a sense of structure and meaning in the midst of loss.

- **Continuing Bonds**: Finding ways to maintain a connection with what was lost, such as through remembrance or legacy activities, can be a comforting aspect of adapting to loss.

Transformation and Growth Post-Grief

The period following intense grief can be marked by a renewed sense of growth and transformation.

- **New Perspectives on Life**: The experience of loss can lead to a changed perspective on life, often with a greater appreciation for the present moment and a redefined sense of purpose.

- **Integration into Personal Narrative**: Integrating the experience of loss and grief into one's personal narrative is a key aspect of evolving, contributing to a more profound understanding of the self and life.

In the continuous journey of becoming, grief, as a response to loss and trauma, is not merely a hurdle to overcome but a profound aspect of personal transformation. While challenging, it can lead to significant personal growth, deeper self-awareness, and an enhanced capacity for empathy and connection. Embracing grief as an integral part of the evolving self enables individuals to navigate through loss with resilience, finding renewed meaning and purpose in its aftermath. The journey through grief, though marked by pain, is also a testament to the enduring strength and adaptability of the human spirit in the face of life's most profound challenges.

Healing and Moving On:

The journey of the evolving self, in its multifaceted and dynamic nature, often traverses the difficult terrains of loss and trauma. These experiences, while deeply challenging, also hold the potential for profound healing and growth. Moving on from such experiences is not about forgetting or leaving behind, but about integrating these experiences into the fabric of one's being and using them as a catalyst for transformation.

The Complexity of Healing

Healing from loss and trauma is a deeply personal and non-linear process.

- **Unique Responses**: Every individual's response to trauma and loss is unique, influenced by personal history, resilience, and the nature of the experience.

- **Holistic Healing**: Healing encompasses the physical, emotional, psychological, and sometimes spiritual aspects of a person. It's about restoring balance and well-being across all these dimensions.

Stages of Healing

While not linear or uniform, several stages are commonly observed in the healing journey.

- **Shock and Denial**: Initial reactions to trauma or loss often include shock and denial, serving as psychological protection against overwhelming emotions.

- **Pain and Grieving**: As the shock wears off, the pain of the loss becomes more apparent. Grieving is a natural and necessary part of the healing process.

- **Adjustment and Adaptation**: Over time, there is a gradual movement towards adjusting and adapting to life without what was lost or how trauma has changed one's life.

- **Integration and Growth**: Ultimately, healing involves integrating the experience into one's life story, leading to personal growth and a renewed sense of self.

Strategies for Healing and Moving On

Several strategies can facilitate the process of healing and moving forward.

- **Seeking Support**: Engaging with supportive networks, whether friends, family, or professional counselors, can provide comfort and guidance.

- **Expressive Outlets**: Finding ways to express emotions and thoughts, such as through journaling, art, or music, can be therapeutic and cathartic.

- **Self-Care Practices**: Prioritizing self-care, including physical health, rest, and engaging in comforting activities, is crucial for recovery.

- **Mindfulness and Meditation**: Practices like mindfulness and meditation can help manage stress, ground emotions, and promote psychological healing.

The Role of Resilience and Hope

Resilience and hope are vital elements in the journey of healing.

- **Building Resilience**: Resilience involves developing the psychological tools to cope with and adapt to challenges. This can be built over time through various practices and experiences.

- **Maintaining Hope**: Holding onto hope, even in the face of despair, can be a powerful motivator in moving forward. It's about finding things to look forward to and believing in the possibility of a positive future.

Redefining Identity Post-Trauma

Loss and trauma can lead to a redefinition of one's identity and worldview.

- **New Self-Understanding**: As individuals heal, they often gain new insights into who they are, their strengths, and their values.

- **Altered Worldview**: Experiences of trauma and loss can change one's perspective on life, relationships, and the world, sometimes leading to a deeper appreciation for life and a reevaluation of priorities.

Conclusion:

Healing from loss and trauma is an integral part of the evolving self's journey. It is a process that not only involves working through pain and grief but also encompasses building resilience, redefining identity, and cultivating hope. As individuals navigate this path, they can discover new depths of strength and understanding within themselves. Moving on, thus, becomes a process of integrating and transforming experiences of loss and trauma into pillars of personal growth and self-discovery. In this journey, the evolving self learns to embrace life's complexities, finding a renewed sense of purpose and meaning in the aftermath of its greatest challenges.

PART V: BEYOND THE INDIVIDUAL

Chapter 16: The Evolving Relationship

In the tapestry of personal growth, the evolving relationship – with oneself and others – is a central thread. Relationships, in all their complexity, not only reflect who we are at various stages of our journey but also actively shape our evolving self. This narrative explores the dynamics of relationships in the context of personal development, highlighting how they transform and contribute to our continuous journey of becoming.

The Mirror of Relationships

Relationships act as mirrors, reflecting aspects of ourselves that we may not otherwise see.

- **Self-Reflection and Growth**: Interactions with others can reveal personal strengths, weaknesses, and areas for growth. They often bring to light hidden aspects of our character.

- **Feedback and Perspective**: Constructive feedback from others, be it from a partner, friend, or family member, can provide valuable insights and alternative perspectives.

The Evolving Self in Intimate Relationships

Intimate relationships, in particular, play a significant role in personal evolution.

- **Learning and Adapting**: These relationships demand learning and adaptation. They challenge us to grow in empathy, understanding, and emotional intelligence.

- **Conflict and Resolution**: Navigating conflicts in intimate relationships can lead to deeper understanding and improved communication skills.

- **Shared Growth**: A healthy relationship involves growing together, with each partner supporting the other's personal growth and goals.

Friendships and Social Connections

Friendships and broader social connections also contribute significantly to the evolving self.

- **Support and Belonging**: Friends provide emotional support, a sense of belonging, and a safe space to share and explore different facets of our personality.

- **Influence and Inspiration**: Friends can also inspire us, challenge our thinking, and encourage us to step out of our comfort zones.

Relationship with Oneself

Central to all external relationships is the relationship with oneself.

- **Self-Awareness and Acceptance**: Understanding and accepting oneself is crucial for authentic interactions with others. It involves acknowledging one's needs, desires, and boundaries.

- **Self-Compassion and Growth**: Cultivating self-compassion and a commitment to personal growth creates a solid foundation for all other relationships.

Changing Dynamics Over Time

As individuals evolve, so do their relationships.

- **Transforming Needs and Roles**: As people grow, their needs, expectations, and roles in relationships may change, requiring adjustments and renegotiations.

- **Letting Go and Forming New Bonds**: Sometimes personal growth involves letting go of relationships that no longer serve or reflect one's evolving self and forming new connections that align better with one's current path.

Navigating Challenges in Relationships

Challenges in relationships are inevitable and can be catalysts for growth.

- **Conflict as Opportunity**: Constructive conflict can be an opportunity for personal growth, promoting deeper understanding and strengthening bonds.

- **Resilience and Empathy**: Overcoming relational challenges builds resilience and enhances empathy, key components of emotional intelligence.

In the continuous journey of becoming, relationships play a pivotal role. They are not just companions on the journey but active agents in shaping the evolving self. Through the give-and-take of relationships, individuals learn about themselves, others, and the complexities of human interactions. The dynamics of evolving relationships – the challenges, joys, adjustments, and learning they bring – are integral to personal growth and self-discovery. Embracing these relationships, in all their forms, as part of the journey of becoming, enriches the personal evolution process, leading to a more connected, empathetic, and fulfilling life.

Personal Growth in Partnerships:

In the intricate journey of self-development, partnerships play a profound role in shaping and reflecting our evolving selves. Romantic partnerships, in particular, are not just unions of affection but can also be powerful catalysts for personal growth and self-discovery. This narrative delves into how romantic relationships contribute to the evolving self, highlighting the dynamics of personal growth within the context of a partnership.

The Dance of Intimacy and Individuality

Partnerships often navigate the delicate balance between intimacy and individuality, a dynamic central to personal growth.

- **Mutual Support and Individual Goals**: Healthy relationships support mutual growth while respecting individual goals and aspirations.

- **Interdependency vs. Codependency**: Striking a balance between interdependency, where partners support each other without losing their sense of self, and avoiding codependency is crucial for personal and relational health.

Communication as a Tool for Growth

Effective communication in partnerships is not just about resolving conflicts; it's a pathway to deeper understanding and personal development.

- **Understanding and Empathy**: Open, honest communication fosters understanding and empathy, essential for emotional growth.

- **Conflict Resolution**: Learning to navigate conflicts constructively can enhance problem-solving skills and emotional intelligence.

- **Reflective Listening**: This skill not only aids in resolving misunderstandings but also promotes a deeper understanding of one's own and the partner's emotional landscape.

The Mirror of Relationship

Romantic partnerships often act as mirrors, reflecting aspects of our personalities that we may not easily see.

- **Revealing Blind Spots**: Partners can help reveal blind spots in our self-perception, offering opportunities for self-awareness and growth.

- **Triggering Growth**: Relationships can trigger growth by exposing vulnerabilities, insecurities, and unresolved issues, prompting personal development.

Challenges as Catalysts for Growth

The challenges encountered in partnerships can serve as important catalysts for personal growth.

- **Learning from Differences**: Navigating differences in opinion, lifestyle, or background can broaden perspectives and foster tolerance and flexibility.

- **Overcoming Adversity Together**: Facing and overcoming challenges together can strengthen resilience and deepen the bond.

Nurturing Self and Relationship

Personal growth in partnerships requires nurturing both the relationship and the individual selves within it.

- **Balancing Togetherness and Separateness**: Ensuring that each partner has space for personal pursuits and self-care is as important as nurturing the relationship.

- **Continuous Learning and Adaptation**: As individuals evolve, so does the relationship, necessitating continuous learning and adaptation from both partners.

The Evolving Dynamics of Long-Term Relationships

In long-term relationships, the evolution of each partner can transform the dynamics of the partnership.

- **Realigning with Life Transitions**: Major life transitions, such as career changes, parenthood, or aging, require realignment and adjustment in the relationship.

- **Renewed Understanding**: Long-term partnerships offer the opportunity to deepen understanding and appreciation for each other's evolving selves.

The evolving relationship in the context of a romantic partnership is a synergistic element of personal growth. It offers a unique confluence of intimacy, challenge, and support that can significantly propel the journey of becoming. In navigating the complexities of a shared life, individuals find opportunities for profound self-discovery and development. A healthy partnership not only survives but thrives on the individual growth of each partner, evolving into a deeper, more meaningful union. In this dance of growing together while nurturing individuality, the evolving relationship becomes a testament to the transformative power of love and partnership in the journey of personal evolution.

The Dynamic of Changing Together:

In the personal evolution, the dynamics of a relationship play a pivotal role. As individuals grow and evolve, so do their relationships. This narrative explores the concept of evolving relationships, focusing on the dynamic of changing together – how two individuals in a relationship can grow both individually and as a couple, navigating the complexities of life's changes side by side.

The Interplay of Individual Growth and Relationship Evolution

The evolution of a relationship is deeply intertwined with the personal growth of each partner.

- **Mutual Influence**: Individual changes inevitably influence the relationship. As each partner grows, learns, and changes, so does the dynamic of the relationship.

- **Harmonizing Growth**: The challenge and beauty of a relationship lie in harmonizing these individual growth paths, ensuring that while each person evolves, the relationship does too.

Communication: The Lifeline of Evolving Relationships

Effective communication is the lifeline that sustains the growth of a relationship.

- **Navigating Change Through Dialogue**: Open, honest, and empathetic communication helps partners understand and support each other's growth trajectories.

- **Resolving Conflicts Constructively**: The ability to resolve conflicts constructively, acknowledging and respecting differences, is key to growing together rather than apart.

The Challenge of Change

Change, although inevitable, can be challenging for relationships.

- **Adapting to New Roles and Identities**: Life events like career changes, parenthood, or retirement can lead to new roles and identities for each partner, requiring adjustments within the relationship.

- **Maintaining Connection Amidst Change**: Keeping the emotional connection strong amidst these changes is essential for the relationship to thrive.

Support Systems and External Influences

External factors play a significant role in how relationships evolve.

- **Influence of External Stressors**: Factors such as financial stress, work pressure, or societal expectations can impact how couples grow and change together.

- **Relying on Support Systems**: Strong support systems, including family, friends, and community, can provide stability and perspective as couples navigate changes.

Growing Together Through Shared Experiences

Shared experiences, both challenging and joyful, can be a catalyst for collective growth.

- **Creating and Sharing New Experiences**: Actively creating and sharing experiences, whether through travel, hobbies, or shared goals, can strengthen the bond and foster mutual growth.

- **Learning from Each Other**: Partners can learn from each other's strengths, perspectives, and coping mechanisms, enriching their own personal growth.

The Role of Flexibility and Compromise

Flexibility and compromise are crucial in adapting to each other's changes.

- **Embracing Change**: Being open to and accepting of changes in one's partner is crucial for the relationship to evolve.

- **Balancing Individual Needs with Relationship Goals**: Striking a balance between individual needs and the goals of the relationship is key to growing together harmoniously.

Conclusion:

The evolving relationship is a testament to the beauty and complexity of changing together. It requires patience, understanding, and a commitment to both individual and collective growth. As partners navigate their personal journeys of becoming, they also craft a shared journey – one that is enriched by each individual's evolution. This dynamic of evolving together is not just about enduring life's changes but about embracing them as opportunities for deepening the relationship and discovering new dimensions of love and companionship. In this dance of individual and collective growth, the evolving relationship becomes a living, breathing entity, reflective of the beauty and dynamism of human connections.

Chapter 17: Communities in Transformation

The evolving self does not occur in isolation but within the broader context of communities undergoing their own transformations. Communities, whether defined by geography, interest, culture, or shared experiences, significantly influence and are influenced by the personal growth of their members. This narrative explores the dynamic interplay between individual evolution and community transformation, underscoring the significance of communal contexts in shaping the journey of becoming.

The Role of Community in Personal Evolution

Communities play a multifaceted role in the personal development of individuals.

- **Support and Belonging**: Communities provide a sense of belonging and support, offering a network where individuals can share experiences, gain encouragement, and find understanding.

- **Shared Learning and Growth**: They serve as spaces for shared learning, where collective wisdom and diverse perspectives can catalyze personal growth and broaden understanding.

- **Reflection of Cultural and Social Norms**: Communities often reflect the cultural and social norms that shape individual values and beliefs, influencing personal development trajectories.

Impact of Individual Change on Community Dynamics

Just as communities influence individuals, the personal growth of individuals can impact the dynamics of their communities.

- **Agents of Change**: Individuals who undergo significant personal growth can become agents of change within their communities, inspiring others and introducing new ideas and perspectives.

- **Shifting Community Norms**: As individuals evolve, they can challenge and shift community norms and values, contributing to the community's transformation.

Communities in Transition

Communities themselves are in a constant state of flux and transformation, responding to external and internal influences.

- **Response to Societal Changes**: Communities adapt and transform in response to broader societal changes, such as technological advancements, economic shifts, or social movements.

- **Internal Evolution**: Communities also evolve from within, as the needs, aspirations, and compositions of their members change over time.

The Synergy of Individual and Community Growth

The relationship between individual growth and community transformation is synergistic.

- **Collective Empowerment**: As individuals grow, they can contribute more effectively to their communities, leading to collective empowerment and progress.

- **Enhanced Resilience**: Strong, evolving communities enhance the resilience of their members, providing a safety net during personal challenges and transitions.

Challenges and Opportunities

The interplay between individual evolution and community transformation presents both challenges and opportunities.

- **Navigating Differences**: Balancing personal growth with communal harmony can be challenging, especially when individual changes diverge from community norms.

- **Opportunities for Leadership**: Personal development can open opportunities for leadership within communities, allowing individuals to guide and influence communal growth.

The evolving self and the transforming community are deeply interconnected, each influencing and enriching the other. Recognizing and embracing this interconnectedness is key to a holistic approach to personal development. As individuals grow, they contribute to the evolution of their communities, which in turn provide the context, support, and challenges necessary for continued personal growth. This dynamic interplay underscores the importance of nurturing both personal development and community engagement, as each plays a crucial role in the broader journey of becoming. In this interconnected path, the evolving self and the transforming community co-create a landscape of shared growth, resilience, and collective progress.

The Power of Collective Evolution:

The journey of personal evolution is intricately linked to the transformation of communities. Collective evolution, the process where communities grow and change, profoundly impacts individual growth. This narrative explores how the evolving self is not just an isolated entity but part of a larger tapestry of community evolution, highlighting the power of collective growth and transformation.

The Interdependence of Self and Community

The relationship between the individual and the community is fundamentally interdependent.

- **Influence of Community**: The values, beliefs, and norms of a community deeply influence the personal development of its members.

- **Individual Contributions**: Conversely, each individual's growth, insights, and actions contribute to the collective evolution of their community.

Collective Evolution in Action

Communities evolve through shared experiences, challenges, and the collective pursuit of goals.

- **Shared Experiences**: Common experiences, whether challenges like natural disasters or achievements like community projects, foster a collective identity and sense of purpose.

- **Cultural and Social Shifts**: Communities transform as they navigate cultural and social shifts, adapting to new ideas and integrating diverse perspectives.

The Role of Community Leadership

Leadership within communities plays a critical role in guiding collective evolution.

- **Visionary Leadership**: Effective community leaders can inspire collective action and nurture a shared vision for the future.

- **Empowering Others**: Leaders who empower members to contribute their skills and ideas foster a sense of agency and participation in the community's evolution.

Challenges in Collective Evolution

As communities transform, they face various challenges that can impact individual members.

- **Resistance to Change**: Communities, like individuals, can experience resistance to change, especially when it challenges long-held beliefs or traditions.

- **Navigating Conflict**: Differences in opinions and interests can lead to conflicts, requiring careful navigation to maintain community cohesion.

The Power of Collective Action

Collective evolution is often driven by the power of collaborative action.

- **Grassroots Movements**: Grassroots initiatives can bring about significant change, illustrating the power of collective action in shaping societal norms and policies.

- **Community Projects**: Local projects, whether environmental, educational, or social, can serve as catalysts for community transformation and individual growth.

Learning and Growing Together

Collective evolution provides opportunities for shared learning and mutual growth.

- **Exchange of Ideas and Skills**: Communities are hubs for the exchange of ideas, knowledge, and skills, enriching the personal growth of members.

- **Collective Wisdom**: The combined experiences and insights of a community constitute a form of collective wisdom that can guide individual and communal decisions.

The Ripple Effect of Community Transformation

The transformation of a community can have a ripple effect, influencing broader societal change.

- **Influencing Larger Systems**: Transformative community actions can influence larger social, political, and economic systems.

- **Inspiring Other Communities**: One community's successful transformation can serve as a model and inspiration for others.

In the evolving journey of the self, recognizing and embracing the role of community and collective evolution is crucial. Individual growth and community transformation are deeply interconnected, each fueling and shaping the other. By engaging in and contributing to the collective evolution of their communities, individuals can find a richer, more meaningful path in their personal development. The power of collective evolution lies not just in the achievement of communal goals but in the shared journey of growth, learning, and transformation that it fosters. In this journey, the evolving self finds a sense of belonging, purpose, and a deeper connection to the larger story of human progress and development.

Societal Shifts and Their Impact on the Individual:

The journey of the evolving self occurs within a broader societal context, where significant shifts and transformations continuously reshape the community landscape. These societal changes, whether technological, cultural, economic, or political, have profound impacts on the individual's personal development journey. This narrative explores how societal shifts influence the evolving self, molding perceptions, values, and life paths.

Societal Shifts and Community Dynamics

Societal changes often lead to transformations within communities, affecting their norms, values, and structures.

- **Cultural Evolution**: Shifts in cultural norms and values can redefine what is considered acceptable or desirable, influencing individual beliefs and behaviors.

- **Economic and Technological Changes**: Economic fluctuations and technological advancements can alter lifestyles, work patterns, and communication, impacting personal and professional development.

- **Political and Social Movements**: Political shifts and social movements can challenge existing power structures and ideologies, creating new paradigms for individuals to navigate.

The Individual Within a Shifting Society

As society changes, individuals must adapt and evolve within this new context.

- **Identity and Belonging**: Societal shifts can impact personal identity and the sense of belonging, especially when they affect cultural or community ties.

- **Opportunities and Challenges**: Changes in society can open new opportunities for growth and development but can also present challenges and uncertainties.

- **Resilience and Adaptability**: The ability to adapt to societal changes is crucial for personal resilience and continued growth.

The Role of Technology and Digital Transformation

In the digital age, technology plays a significant role in societal shifts and, consequently, in personal development.

- **Digital Connectivity**: The rise of digital communication and social media has transformed how individuals connect, share, and learn, impacting social dynamics and relationships.

- **Information Access and Learning**: The vast access to information and learning resources can enhance personal development but also presents challenges around information overload and digital distraction.

- **Work-Life Balance**: Technological advancements have changed work patterns, influencing work-life balance and personal priorities.

Navigating Societal Shifts

Individuals must develop strategies to navigate the complexities of societal shifts.

- **Continuous Learning**: Staying informed and engaged with societal changes is essential for personal and professional adaptability.

- **Critical Thinking**: Developing critical thinking skills is crucial to navigate the influx of information and differing perspectives brought about by societal changes.

- **Emotional Intelligence**: Cultivating emotional intelligence helps in managing the psychological and emotional impacts of societal shifts.

The Impact on Relationships and Community Engagement

Societal shifts also influence personal relationships and community engagement.

- **Shifting Relationship Dynamics**: Changes in societal norms can affect family structures, friendship dynamics, and romantic relationships.

- **Community Involvement**: Engaging with community initiatives related to societal changes can provide a sense of purpose and connection.

Societal Shifts as Catalysts for Personal Growth

While challenging, societal shifts can act as catalysts for profound personal growth.

- **Expanding Perspectives**: Exposure to new ideas and cultures broadens perspectives, enhancing personal development.

- **Personal and Social Responsibility**: Navigating societal changes often involves reevaluating one's role and responsibility in society, leading to more conscientious and empathetic actions.

Conclusion:

In the evolving journey of the self, societal shifts play a critical role, influencing and shaping individual paths. As society transforms, so do the communities and individuals within it, creating a dynamic interplay between personal development and societal change. By embracing these changes, adapting to new realities, and finding ways to contribute positively, individuals can navigate their personal evolution in a way that aligns with the broader narrative of societal transformation. This interconnected path highlights the importance of understanding and engaging with societal shifts as integral to the journey of becoming, offering opportunities for enrichment, challenge, and growth.

Chapter 18: Legacy and Generational Influence

The evolving self is deeply interwoven with the concepts of legacy and generational influence. Our personal growth is not just shaped by our immediate experiences but also by the rich tapestry of our ancestry and the legacy we aim to leave for future generations. This narrative explores how legacy and generational influences contribute to and enrich the continuous journey of becoming, shaping our identity, values, and aspirations.

The Impact of Generational Influence

Generational influence plays a significant role in shaping our early understanding of the world and ourselves.

- **Cultural and Familial Heritage**: Our family's history, culture, and traditions provide a backdrop against which our personal identity is formed.

- **Inherited Beliefs and Values**: We often inherit a set of beliefs, values, and norms from our forebears, which can guide or challenge our personal growth journey.

- **Intergenerational Stories and Lessons**: The stories, struggles, and triumphs of previous generations can inspire and influence our life choices and pathways.

Understanding and Reevaluating Inherited Legacies

As we evolve, we often reevaluate and reinterpret the legacy passed down to us.

- **Personalization of Legacy**: We might embrace, adapt, or even reject certain aspects of our inherited legacy as we develop our unique identity and values.

- **Healing Intergenerational Trauma**: Part of personal growth can involve recognizing and healing intergenerational traumas, breaking cycles that may have been passed down.

- **Building Upon the Past**: We can also choose to build upon the positive aspects of our generational legacy, carrying forward the strengths and lessons learned.

The Creation of Personal Legacy

Personal legacy is not just about what we leave behind; it's about how we live and influence the world in our lifetimes.

- **Impact on Others**: Our interactions, relationships, and contributions to society collectively form the legacy we create.

- **Living with Intention**: Conscious choices and living with intention in alignment with our values contribute to the legacy we are actively creating.

- **Mentorship and Guidance**: Passing on knowledge, wisdom, and support to younger generations or peers is a vital part of leaving a meaningful legacy.

Generational Dynamics in Modern Times

In today's rapidly changing world, generational dynamics are evolving, impacting the journey of becoming.

- **Technological and Societal Shifts**: Rapid technological advancements and societal shifts can create distinct experiences and perspectives between generations.

- **Bridging Generational Gaps**: Understanding and bridging these generational gaps can enhance personal growth and lead to richer, more diverse perspectives.

The Role of Reflection in Legacy Building

Reflection is a critical tool in understanding and shaping one's legacy.

- **Reflecting on Life's Impact**: Regular reflection helps in assessing the impact of one's actions and decisions on others and on future generations.

- **Contemplating Long-Term Influence**: Considering the long-term effects of our actions on future generations can guide more sustainable and ethical choices.

Legacy and generational influence are integral to the evolving self. They provide a context from which we emerge and against which we define ourselves. As we journey through life, we not only carry the legacy of our ancestors but also actively craft our own. This process is not static but dynamic, allowing room for reevaluation, growth, and new creation. By embracing and contributing to this generational continuum, we participate in a cycle that transcends our individual existence, becoming part of a larger, ongoing story of human development and progression. In the end, understanding and shaping our legacy becomes a key aspect of our journey of becoming, adding depth and meaning to our personal evolution.

Passing Down Wisdom:

The concept of legacy within the framework of the evolving self extends beyond material inheritance, encompassing the rich tapestry of wisdom, values, experiences, and insights that are passed down through generations. This transmission of wisdom is a vital aspect of both personal and collective evolution, creating a bridge between the past, present, and future. This narrative explores the role of passing down wisdom in shaping the evolving self and its significance in the context of generational influence.

The Essence of Wisdom in Legacy

Wisdom, accrued through the lived experiences and reflections of individuals, forms the core of what is often passed down through generations.

- **Shared Experiences and Lessons**: Life lessons, derived from personal experiences, triumphs, and failures, constitute a significant part of the wisdom that is shared.

- **Cultural and Moral Values**: Along with practical knowledge, cultural beliefs, moral values, and ethical frameworks are often conveyed, shaping the character and worldview of subsequent generations.

Mechanisms of Transmitting Wisdom

The transmission of wisdom occurs through various mechanisms, both formal and informal.

- **Storytelling and Oral Traditions**: Stories, anecdotes, and oral traditions are powerful ways to impart wisdom, making abstract or complex lessons more relatable and memorable.

- **Modeling and Mentorship**: Wisdom is often passed down through role modeling and mentorship, where behaviors, attitudes, and skills are learned through observation and guidance.

- **Written Works and Artifacts**: Letters, journals, books, and other artifacts can serve as tangible vessels of wisdom, offering insights and guidance.

The Impact of Wisdom on the Evolving Self

Receiving and integrating wisdom from previous generations profoundly impacts the journey of self-evolution.

- **Guidance and Direction**: Wisdom from past generations can provide guidance, helping individuals navigate life's challenges and make informed decisions.

- **Sense of Identity and Continuity**: This shared wisdom contributes to a sense of identity and belonging, linking individuals to their familial and cultural heritage.

- **Adaptation and Growth**: While some wisdom is timeless, the process of adapting and reinterpreting this knowledge in contemporary contexts is key to personal growth and relevance.

The Responsibility of Passing Down Wisdom

As individuals evolve, they become custodians of wisdom, responsible for passing it down to future generations.

- **Selective Transmission**: Part of this responsibility involves discerning which aspects of wisdom and knowledge are beneficial and relevant to pass down.

- **Updating and Expanding Wisdom**: It also involves expanding upon this wisdom based on one's own experiences and learnings, ensuring its applicability in a changing world.

- **Empowering Future Generations**: The ultimate goal of passing down wisdom is to empower future generations, equipping them with the knowledge, skills, and values to lead fulfilling lives.

Challenges in the Modern Context

In the contemporary world, the transmission of wisdom faces unique challenges.

- **Rapid Societal Changes**: The fast pace of technological and societal changes can create a disconnect between traditional wisdom and modern realities.

- **Overload of Information**: The sheer volume of information available today can sometimes overshadow the nuanced, reflective wisdom of past generations.

Passing down wisdom is a crucial component of the evolving self and its legacy, forming an invisible thread that connects generations. It is a dynamic process, requiring adaptation, discernment, and a conscious effort to preserve and impart valuable knowledge and insights. As individuals navigate their personal journeys of becoming, they not only benefit from the wisdom of their predecessors but also contribute to this continuum of knowledge, shaping the legacy for future generations. In this way, wisdom becomes more than just a heritage; it transforms into a living, evolving entity, integral to the collective journey of human growth and development.

The Role of the Elder in Modern Times:

In the context of legacy and generational influence, the role of elders in modern times presents a unique dimension to the evolving self. Traditionally revered as custodians of wisdom and experience, elders in contemporary society navigate a landscape that is rapidly changing, often challenging the conventional perceptions of aging and wisdom. This narrative examines the evolving role of elders and their impact on individual and collective growth in modern times.

The Evolving Perception of Elders

The perception of elders and their societal roles have undergone significant transformations.

- **From Traditional to Modern Roles**: Once viewed predominantly as repositories of wisdom and guidance, elders in modern societies are redefining their roles, balancing traditional wisdom with contemporary challenges.

- **Active Participation in Society**: Increasingly, elders are participating actively in various sectors, including the workforce, education, and community leadership, challenging stereotypes about aging.

The Wisdom of Experience

Despite societal changes, the wisdom that elders bring, born of experience and reflection, remains invaluable.

- **Life Lessons and Experiences**: The experiences accumulated over a lifetime, including successes and failures, offer profound lessons for younger generations.

- **Guidance and Mentorship**: Elders often provide guidance and mentorship, drawing on their life experiences to offer insights and advice.

Intergenerational Relationships and Learning

Elders play a crucial role in fostering intergenerational relationships and learning.

- **Bridging Generational Gaps**: By sharing their experiences and perspectives, elders can help bridge the gap between different generations, fostering understanding and empathy.

- **Role Models of Lifelong Learning**: Elders who continue to learn and adapt serve as powerful role models, illustrating that personal growth and development are lifelong processes.

The Challenge of Modernity for Elders

Elders face unique challenges in adapting to the rapid pace of change in modern society.

- **Technological Advancements**: Keeping pace with technological advancements can be challenging for some elders, yet many show remarkable adaptability and willingness to learn.

- **Changing Family Dynamics**: With shifts in family structures and dynamics, the role of elders within families has also evolved, sometimes leading to feelings of isolation or underappreciation.

Elders as Keepers of History and Culture

Elders serve as living links to the past, preserving history and culture.

- **Cultural Preservation**: Through storytelling and the sharing of traditions, elders play a key role in preserving cultural heritage.

- **Historical Context**: Their firsthand accounts of historical events provide valuable context and insights, enriching the collective understanding of the past.

The Role of Elders in Community Building

Elders contribute significantly to community building and social cohesion.

- **Community Engagement and Volunteerism**: Many elders actively engage in community service and volunteerism, contributing to social welfare and cohesion.

- **Wisdom in Community Decision-Making**: Their insights and experience can be invaluable in community decision-making processes, offering balance and depth.

Conclusion:

In modern times, the role of the elder is both a testament to the enduring value of experience and wisdom and a reflection of the capacity for continuous growth and adaptation. As integral parts of the tapestry of generational evolution, elders not only contribute to the legacy of knowledge and culture but also exemplify the enduring journey of the evolving self. Their active engagement in modern society challenges preconceived notions about aging and underscores the importance of intergenerational dialogue in the collective journey of human development. In recognizing and valuing the evolving role of elders, society enriches its understanding of the continuous journey of becoming, across all stages of life.

APPENDICES

A. Recommended Reading and Resources:

In the journey of self-evolution, knowledge and insight gained from external sources play a pivotal role. The Recommended Reading and Resources appendix serves as a curated collection of materials that enlighten, challenge, and support the evolving self. These resources are not just tools for information but catalysts for growth, understanding, and transformation.

Recommended Reading

Books and written materials offer diverse perspectives and deep insights into the nature of personal growth and human experience.

- **Self-Help and Personal Development**: Titles like "The 7 Habits of Highly Effective People" by Stephen Covey and "Awaken the Giant Within" by Tony Robbins provide strategies for personal growth and self-improvement.

- **Psychology and Mindfulness**: Works such as "Man's Search for Meaning" by Viktor Frankl and "Wherever You Go, There You Are" by Jon Kabat-Zinn offer psychological insights and mindfulness practices.

- **Biographies and Memoirs**: Inspirational stories of individuals, like "The Diary of a Young Girl" by Anne Frank or "Long Walk to Freedom" by Nelson Mandela, can provide motivation and perspective.

- **Philosophy and Spirituality**: Books like "The Alchemist" by Paulo Coelho or "The Power of Now" by Eckhart Tolle explore spiritual and philosophical insights on life's journey.

Online Resources and Websites

The internet is a vast repository of resources for personal development, offering a range of perspectives and tools.

- **Educational Platforms**: Websites like Coursera, Udemy, or Khan Academy offer courses on various topics, including personal development, psychology, and skill-building.

- **Mindfulness and Meditation Apps**: Apps such as Headspace or Calm provide guided meditation and mindfulness exercises, beneficial for mental well-being.

- **Blogs and Articles**: Online platforms like Medium, TED Talks, or the Harvard Business Review blog offer insightful articles and talks on a wide array of subjects related to personal growth.

Podcasts and Audio Resources

For auditory learners, podcasts and audiobooks can be a convenient and engaging way to access information.

- **Inspirational Podcasts**: Shows like "The Tim Ferriss Show" or "Oprah's SuperSoul Conversations" feature interviews with thought leaders and experts in various fields.

- **Audiobooks**: Many find listening to audiobooks a convenient way to consume literature, with platforms like Audible offering a wide range of titles.

Supportive Communities and Groups

Joining communities or groups can provide support, encouragement, and shared learning.

- **Local Meetup Groups**: Platforms like Meetup.com can help find local groups interested in personal development, mindfulness, or specific hobbies.

- **Online Forums and Social Media Groups**: Online communities, found on platforms like Reddit or Facebook, offer spaces to discuss ideas, challenges, and achievements with like-minded individuals.

Workshops and Seminars

Participating in workshops and seminars can provide immersive learning experiences.

- **Personal Development Workshops**: Workshops focusing on specific areas of personal growth, such as leadership, communication, or emotional intelligence, offer practical learning.

- **Retreats and Conferences**: Attending retreats or conferences on topics like mindfulness, wellness, or spirituality can be deeply enriching experiences.

B. Exercises and Practices for Personal Growth:

Personal growth is a dynamic and ongoing process that requires active engagement and practice. Appendix B focuses on exercises and practices specifically designed to facilitate personal growth, offering a practical guide to individuals on their journey of becoming. These exercises and practices are tools to deepen self-awareness, enhance skills, and foster a mindset conducive to continuous development.

Mindfulness and Meditation Practices

In the realm of personal development, mindfulness and meditation are fundamental practices.

- **Daily Mindfulness Exercises**: Incorporating mindfulness into daily routines, like mindful eating, walking, or breathing exercises, helps in staying present and aware.

- **Guided Meditation**: Using guided meditation sessions, available through apps or online resources, can assist in achieving relaxation and mental clarity.

- **Journaling for Mindfulness**: Keeping a mindfulness journal to reflect on daily experiences and emotions fosters self-awareness and emotional intelligence.

Self-Reflection and Journaling

Self-reflection is crucial for understanding personal motivations, feelings, and aspirations.

- **Daily Reflections**: Setting aside time each day to reflect on experiences, challenges, and learnings.

- **Gratitude Journaling**: Maintaining a gratitude journal to regularly document things one is thankful for, enhancing positivity and well-being.

- **Goal-Setting Exercises**: Using journaling to set, review, and track progress towards personal goals.

Emotional Intelligence Development

Developing emotional intelligence is key to personal and interpersonal growth.

- **Empathy Practices**: Engaging in exercises that enhance empathy, such as active listening or perspective-taking activities.

- **Emotion Tracking**: Keeping a record of emotional responses to understand triggers and patterns better.

- **Conflict Resolution Role-Playing**: Practicing conflict resolution through role-playing scenarios to improve communication and problem-solving skills.

Skill Development and Learning

Continuous learning and skill development are essential aspects of personal growth.

- **Online Courses and Workshops**: Enrolling in online courses or workshops on topics of interest or areas for improvement.

- **Reading and Research**: Regularly reading books, articles, or research papers to stay informed and expand knowledge.

- **Skill-Based Hobbies**: Taking up hobbies or activities that challenge and develop new skills, like learning a musical instrument, a new language, or a craft.

Physical Wellness and Exercise

Physical health is intrinsically linked to mental and emotional well-being.

- **Regular Physical Activity**: Engaging in regular exercise routines, whether it's yoga, jogging, swimming, or gym workouts.

- **Body Awareness Practices**: Participating in activities that increase body awareness and control, such as Pilates, martial arts, or dance.

- **Relaxation Techniques**: Practicing relaxation techniques such as progressive muscle relaxation or deep breathing exercises.

Social Connection and Community Involvement

Building and maintaining social connections and engaging with the community are vital for holistic personal growth.

- **Social Skills Exercises**: Engaging in activities that build social skills, like joining a club, attending community events, or volunteer work.

- **Networking and Relationship Building**: Actively seeking opportunities to build and maintain professional and personal relationships.

- **Mentorship**: Either seeking a mentor for guidance and support or offering mentorship to others.

C. Glossary of Terms:

In the intricate journey of self-evolution, a myriad of concepts and terminologies are encountered, each holding significant meaning and implications for personal growth. Appendix C, the Glossary of Terms, serves as a crucial reference point, providing clear definitions and explanations of key terms related to the evolving self. This glossary aids in deepening understanding and fostering clarity as individuals navigate their path of growth and development.

Glossary of Key Terms in Personal Growth

- **Self-Awareness**:

The conscious knowledge of one's character, feelings, motives, and desires. It is the foundation of personal growth.

- **Mindfulness**:

The practice of maintaining a nonjudgmental state of heightened or complete awareness of one's thoughts, emotions, or experiences on a moment-to-moment basis.

- **Emotional Intelligence (EQ)**:

The ability to identify, assess, and control one's own emotions, the emotions of others, and that of groups.

- **Resilience**:

The capacity to recover quickly from difficulties; emotional strength in facing adversity.

- **Personal Agency**:

The capacity of individuals to act independently and make their own free choices, as opposed to being influenced by external forces.

- **Authenticity**:

The quality of being genuine or true to one's own personality, spirit, or character, despite external pressures.

- **Cognitive Dissonance**:

The state of having inconsistent thoughts, beliefs, or attitudes, especially relating to behavioral decisions and attitude change.

- **Growth Mindset**:

The belief that one's abilities and intelligence can be developed through dedication and hard work.

- **Self-Efficacy**:

The belief in one's ability to succeed in specific situations or accomplish a task.

- **Mind-Body Connection**:

The theory that the mind and body are not distinct entities but interconnected and that psychological factors can affect physical health.

Additional Relevant Terms:

- **Introspection**:

The examination of one's own conscious thoughts and feelings, often as a means of self-analysis.

- **Empathy**:

The ability to understand and share the feelings of another, fostering a sense of connectedness and understanding.

- **Well-being**:

A state characterized by health, happiness, and prosperity; encompasses physical, mental, and emotional health.

- **Mindfulness Meditation**:

A practice where individuals focus their mind on a particular object, thought, or activity to achieve mental clarity and emotional calmness.

- **Lifelong Learning**:

The ongoing, voluntary, and self-motivated pursuit of knowledge for personal or professional reasons.

Conclusion

The Glossary of Terms in Appendix C is an essential resource for anyone on the path of self-evolution. By providing clear definitions and explanations of key concepts, it helps demystify the journey of personal growth, making it more accessible and understandable. This glossary is not only a tool for comprehension but also a companion in the evolving self's journey, offering a linguistic framework to articulate and reflect upon one's experiences and growth. As individuals continue their journey of becoming, this glossary serves as a valuable reference, enriching their understanding and appreciation of the complex and rewarding process of personal development.